IRELAND'S MALAISE

Michael Casey retired early from his position as Chief Economist at the Central Bank of Ireland in order to focus on his writing. He was educated in New Ross, Dublin and the University of Cambridge where he received his PhD in economics. He has worked in the Department of Finance, the Central Bank (with T.K. Whitaker), the University of Cambridge and spent over three years on the Executive Board of the International Monetary Fund in Washington DC where he had the opportunity to study and discuss almost every economy in the world. He contributes regularly to *The Irish Times* and to various literary journals.

IRELAND'S MALAISE

The Troubled Personality of the Irish Economy

MICHAEL CASEY

The Liffey Press

Published by
The Liffey Press
Ashbrook House, 10 Main Street
Raheny, Dublin 5, Ireland
www.theliffeypress.com

A catalogue record of this book is
available from the British Library.

ISBN 978-1-905785-85-8

Printed in Ireland by Colour Books.

CONTENTS

ACKNOWLEDGEMENTS

I wish to thank my economist colleagues in the Central Bank of Ireland who challenged and improved many of the ideas contained in the following pages. I benefited from seminars held by the ESRI, the Dublin Economics Workshop and the Statistical and Social Inquiry Society of Ireland. I was also fortunate to have met interesting people from other countries at various EU and OECD committees.

The three years I spent on the Executive Board of the IMF in Washington, DC were a wonderful learning experience, made even more valuable by contact with the staff of the Federal Reserve Board, the World Bank and the Brookings Institution. The IMF played a critical role in the international financial crisis of the early 1980s; unfortunately, the lessons were soon forgotten by banks and governments. *Plus ça change ...*

Dr. T.K. Whitaker guided my early steps and was the embodiment of the public service ideal – one that, unfortunately, has waned since the era that bears his name. At Cambridge, Professor James Meade, Nobel Laureate, often stressed the role of unconventional ways of solving problems. Professors Roy Geary, Bob O'Connor and Kieran Kennedy of the ESRI were also important early mentors.

Many friends and relatives who run small businesses provided me with insights not readily found in textbooks.

I am most grateful to Jonathan Williams and David Givens, who furnished many astute observations on the manuscript.

I am beholden to Sheila O'Hagan for the tone of critical bonhomie that she fosters at the St. Stephen's Green Writers Group.

The debt owed to my family, who have encouraged my writing endeavours since I took early retirement in 2005, cannot be measured.

All errors and infelicities are, of course, mine.

Michael Casey
September 2010

Dedication

To All My Clans and Absent Leaders

INTRODUCTION

'The greatest discovery of my generation is that a human being can alter his life by altering his attitudes of mind.'
–William James, *Principles of Psychology*, 1890

N
o two economies are the same. One could almost say that every economy has its own personality. Some cultures, for example, are very business-oriented – the United States would be a case in point. Japan and China are also dynamic. Indeed, Chinese people are high performers in other countries, such as Thailand, Indonesia and the Philippines. Capitalism seems to be working well in India but not in Latin America, with the possible exception of Chile.[1] Other societies may be more spiritual or artistic. Tibet is probably the supreme example of other-worldliness. It remains to be seen where Ireland fits on this material–spiritual spectrum.

After all, it is people who run economies. They organise the factors of production through work, management, entrepreneurship and education. They consume, invest, pay taxes, import and export; and they produce goods and services, earn incomes and profits. These are all human activities, yet economists have the habit of referring to these activities in the abstract, for example, 'consumption' or 'investment', instead of referring to the people who engage in the activity – 'consumers' and 'investors'. People are replaced by variables, or by 'economic agents'.

In almost every country in the world, the economy tends to be regarded as something separate and apart from society. In Ireland, there tends to be much more discussion about the economy (as an inanimate entity) than about society, maybe because the latter is more amorphous and less measurable. For example, we often discuss unemployment in statistical terms, while usually ignoring the social and family aspects. Now that we are in the grip of a severe recession, with frightening job losses – in mid-2010 the Live Register stood at almost 453,000 – and falling living standards, it is more important than ever to factor in the social and cultural aspects.

The separation between the economy and society is also unhelpful because it gives the impression that economics is a technical matter, almost a hard science. In fact, it is a social science – relational rather than Newtonian – and because of this, a broad understanding of society, history and community values is essential if we are to form a coherent view about the 'ordinary business of life'. As a shorthand, I will use the term 'culture' to embrace all these wider aspects.

Further evidence of the importance of the broader picture comes from economies like the US, Sweden and Japan, where the manner in which ordinary people and their leaders go about the business of economics is so completely different. This is not owing to the imposition of different economic structures but rather to the free choices made by people with different cultural backgrounds. There is a common humanity present in all societies but there is also a large measure of diversity. And thank goodness for that. Maybe with globalisation and multiculturalism we will someday end up being more or less the same, or 'creolised' as the sociologists call it, but that is a long way off. In the meantime, long live diversity.

A natural scientist studies atoms and molecules but an economist studies people. There is a huge difference. Atoms usually do not 'talk back', but people often do and they can react in perverse and unexpected ways. Hence, there are no fixed laws of economics which can be quantified and applied universally, like the law of gravity, for example. People can second-guess government policies and behave in ways that may even seem irrational at times. Very often an economic solution to a particular problem sows the seeds of its own failure at some point in the future. One could argue that trade unions in the UK were extremely successful on behalf of their own members before the Thatcher era, but they had sown seeds which led to a loss of international competitiveness and, some might say, to their own downfall under the regime of the Iron Lady.

This book tries to make economics more inclusive and to focus more on wider social and cultural issues, which are essential to forming a complete understanding of how economies actually work. This is a necessary precondition for recovering from recession and for assessing longer-term economic growth prospects.

Economists rank close to lawyers and politicians in unpopularity. They are regarded as 'dismal', if not downright depressing. Having referred to them as 'Creeping Jesuses' and 'Loo-Lahs', a former Taoiseach invited some of them to commit suicide. Economists tend to be regarded as right-wing because most of them believe in the market mechanism, which usually excludes wider social concerns.

A few years ago there was a famous exchange on RTE where a 'market' economist told Joe Duffy that people whose homes had been flooded should not receive any compensation from the government because it was up to them to insure their own properties. Joe Duffy pointed out that many of the people concerned would not have been aware of insurance and that others would have been refused cover by insurance companies. The debate was brought to an abrupt end when the economist declared, 'The difference between us, Joe, is that I'm paid to think, whereas you're paid to emote'. There can be little doubt that the majority of listeners sided with Joe Duffy!

The vast majority of policy-makers and commentators did not foresee the present recession. The handful of economists who did see it coming did not predict its extreme gravity. Of course, past trends are not always a good guide to the future, but it does seem as if something else was missing from the analytical tool-box. We really need to know what that is if we are to emerge from recession and get on a sustainable long-term growth path.

The new 'behavioural' economics has brought psychological factors to the fore.[2] This is not before time, though it is still not clear whether or not these psychological insights can be worked into a new general theory as powerful as the existing one of conventional economics. The main problem with this new approach is that the psychological aspects are assumed to have universal validity, whereas a major contention of this book is that economies tend to be culture-specific. In other words, the economy behaves in a way that is consistent with the underlying culture of the country in question. This brings us into difficult territory, dismissed by Hanns Johst with the remark, 'When I hear the word culture, I reach for my revolver'.

No one denies that self-interest is an important motivation in most economic activities. People want value for their hard-earned money. But self-interest is not the only driving force. We need to probe more deeply into cultural factors to gain a true understanding of people in the ordinary business of life. Nearly every politician in Ireland assumed that people would vote for the Lisbon Treaty in the first referendum. After that rejection, the government went into a state of shock and agonised about what had gone wrong. Nothing went wrong. People voted as they wanted to vote; it was an out-of-touch government that got it wrong. The government then went into a long 'period of reflection', almost as if they were in mourning, and hired consultants to try to find out why people had voted 'no'. The second vote on Lisbon also confused politicians, especially the size of the swing from 'no' to 'yes'. It is clear, however, that the sudden and severe recession in Ireland scared people back under the European duvet. Fear can be a powerful motive.

Another example was the unravelling of the first 2009 budget. Again, the government totally misjudged the mood of the people with regard to medical cards for the elderly, student-teacher ratios and the 1 per cent levy. In the 2010 budget the government underestimated the resistance from the public sector to pay cuts. Political scandals, relating to travel expenses and holiday homes, enraged ordinary voters. Government Ministers were stunned in June 2010 when the polls showed a huge swing to Labour. If politicians, who are supposed to have their fingers on the pulse, do not know the mind of the people, how can technical economists hope to make good forecasts or give sound policy advice?

As late as mid-2008, most commentators thought the economy would not go into recession and that the property market and banking system would remain buoyant. The government still spoke about soft landings at worst and berated the few economists who were less optimistic. There was a delusional belief that dramatic downturns could not happen here, and a naive faith in the integrity of property speculators and bankers. It is difficult to understand and predict the economy at the best of times, but it is practically impossible if the broader cultural context is excluded from the analysis.

Has Ireland sown any seeds that might cause difficulties in the future? Is it possible that our fifty-year long policy of attracting fully established foreign companies to these shores may have weakened our own entrepreneurial instincts, or in some way prevented them from developing? Could it be said that we hired other people to run our economy for us because we were not all that interested in doing the humdrum work ourselves? If this rather jaundiced view is even partly correct, what will happen if and when this policy comes to an end? Has our remarkable success sown the seeds of failure in the future, or will our own innate entrepreneurial drive come to the fore? These are the kind of questions that require an understanding of what we are made of, who we are as a people.

The zeitgeist plays a part. For some time the dominant economic philosophy in the West has been one of liberal capitalism. Many commentators believed that this was so successful it would last for ever and a day. Can we be sure of that, especially after the appalling financial meltdown of 2008, a disaster that was caused by unfettered capitalism on Wall Street? Might there be a return to a more egalitarian system in a number of years – with more controls and regulation and more government ownership? How would that suit us? History may or may not move in cycles, but it certainly does not stand still. Culture is not static either, but it changes very slowly.

Most economic textbooks are written by Americans and have led to a one-size-fits-all approach. Whenever teams from the International Monetary Fund (IMF) came to Ireland to review our economy, we used to advise them to put away their textbooks. They found it difficult to do so, since most of them had PhDs from top US universities. On one occasion an IMF team was told that the Irish economy at the time was like a patient suffering from a disorder who needed a set of crutches, even though the disability was entirely psychosomatic. The IMF team was confused and asked if we could get back to the numbers!

Some years ago the chief economist of the World Bank stated that economic growth and development had nothing to do with social and cultural norms, but was completely determined by technical factors such as investment ratios, natural resources, savings ratios and various demographic changes. At the time, I was astounded by this statement, especially by a senior official of the World Bank which dealt with almost 200 different countries. To suggest that the failure of African countries to develop has nothing to do with culture and history is bizarre. If the process of development were merely a question of natural resources and demographics, most African countries should be very well off.

Economic development is such a multi-faceted process that economists have never been able to model it, and most have given up the attempt. A related problem is the emphasis on mathematics. Many younger technical economists, keen to move up the ladder in academia, feel under pressure to impress their peers with mathematical pyrotechnics. Since cultural factors cannot be handled mathematically, it is more convenient to sweep them under the carpet. Fortunately, the World Bank has made something of a comeback and now sends interdisciplinary teams, including anthropologists, to Third World countries.

There was a story doing the rounds in Washington, DC in the late 1980s about a country which had benefited from a major World Bank piped water scheme. The economy and the majority of the people were helped by having water on tap, but there were also some unpredictable effects. The women who used to spend a large part of each day going to the village well, and having a chat with their friends – just as the women in the Bible – suddenly found themselves with more time on their hands. The birth rate rose dramatically. No economist could have predicted that!

Because of tribal *mores*, kinship networks and established practices of bribery, it is difficult for even the most enlightened form of development assistance to bear fruit in sub-Saharan Africa. Even rural development schemes tend to benefit the existing land-owners far more than poor landless people. The fact that women work harder than men – who no longer hunt, but do have legal title to land – is a major constraint on agricultural development. Indeed, many commentators believe that 'institution-building' must be done before the development process can even begin. But if that means changing the culture of the people to a more growth-oriented, Western one, is this not a form of neo-colonialism? Similar problems arise with regard to education. Many African leaders have an inadequate commitment to educating their own people; they might even fear the independent thinking that this may bring. This is perhaps the most serious impediment to growth, and it is not one that can be solved by technical economics.

Another motivation for this book comes from a rich vein of literary criticism in which the effects of our post-colonial past are analysed by writers such as Declan Kiberd, Richard Kearney and Fintan O'Toole.[3] To some extent, this 'cultural studies' approach was also followed by Ronan Fanning and Joe Lee.[4] It seems strange that this valuable analytical framework has never been systematically applied to our economic behaviour on this island.

There was no long unbroken literary tradition, so writers like Joyce and Beckett had to be more inventive because there was no guiding narrative to fall back on, despite the best efforts of Yeats to reinvent a Celtic ethos. Various experiments were tried with differing degrees of success: the Irish revival, romantic nationalism and then the possibly truer rhetoric of resignation associated with a poet like Patrick Kavanagh. All these 'experiments' were, in one way or another, an attempt by an oppressed people to find themselves. Synge's *The Playboy of the Western World* is precisely about this problem of self-conception. Is it possible that, at the start of the second decade of the twenty-first century, we still have not found the economic model that best suits us?

Sociologists and political scientists do not talk so much about alienation anymore. That problem had been associated with assembly-line modes of production. But even today there seems to be some deep-seated discontent or anomie among young people in Ireland which gives rise to binge-drinking, drug-taking, violent actions and suicide. It may be confined to a relatively small group, and hence could be described as a subculture, or even a counterculture, but it is nevertheless hard to explain against the background of an economy that had been performing well for the past fifteen years.

Many of these youngsters may feel they have to prove themselves. They may not have the money, ability or confidence to do this in traditional ways – academically or in terms of earning power. The only way to make a mark is by being tough, or at least by acting tough. The 'hard man' image may still be a part of this subculture.

In general, the psychological insights of Carl Jung are probably the most pertinent to the theme of this book since they include such concepts as archetypes and the collective unconscious. But it must be admitted that when it comes to analysing the behaviour of aggressive male entrepreneurs, Freudian analysis comes more to the fore. In the financial world, and especially on trading floors, phallic metaphors are part of the jargon.

To some extent, the thesis of this book relates to Cardinal Newman's advocacy of a universal approach to knowledge. A good example is the study of man. A doctor understands a certain aspect of man; so do psychologists and philosophers. But we also need physicists, chemists, evolutionary biologists, historians and many other specialists to comprehend fully this one subject. It is this universal or gestalt approach which is lacking in economics.

This book will probably be criticised on the grounds that many of the arguments are based on assertion and opinion, rather than on empirical evidence. First of all, there is very little numerical evidence for this sort of analysis; let's call it discussion instead of analysis. Second, this is not a scientific work, except to the extent that various hypotheses are presented for others to test at some stage, if and when data and appropriate techniques become available. Third, technical economic analysis, though necessary, is often not sufficient. Educated guesswork, backed up by intuition, is usually all we have to go on in a world of uncertainty and human complexity.

One of the great cautionary tales is the collapse of the Long-Term Capital Management hedge fund in the United States. It was set up and run by two Nobel Laureates in economic sciences on the basis of complex mathematical models. But, as Niall Ferguson points out,[5] the models were based on the assumption of a normal probability distribution. After the Russian banking crisis, it became clear that the normal probability function was not appropriate for large, discontinuous changes. The model blew up and the company collapsed.

Moreover, models can be applied only to data which by definition are historical. The fundamental question is whether or not history is always a good guide to the future, and the answer must be 'not always'. A little more humility about the power of techniques would not go amiss. While risk may be measurable to some extent, uncertainty cannot be captured in a mathematical way. The only weapon we have is human judgment, which should be based on some feeling for wider cultural factors.

Another potential criticism of this book is the 'post-modern' one, which states that many of the previous guiding narratives, like the Bible and the works of Karl Marx, are more or less gone from our consciousness and that we live in an age of nihilism. In other words, there is little cultural baggage to influence us one way or the other. This seems to be an extreme theoretical view. We are all products of our past; we can all hear ancestral voices. Most lapsed Catholics still feel an urge to make the sign of the cross when passing a church.

Whether or not other cultures will be imposed on us is unlikely. When a senior member of the English hierarchy recently suggested that Britain should incorporate some aspects of Sharia law into its own legal system, he was roundly denounced even by so-called liberals. The 'McDonald's' culture could spread across the globe, in which case American textbooks may come to fit all economies at some stage in the future. On the other hand, there might be a reaction against this. There could even be a retreat into economic nationalism. (McDonald's pulled out of Iceland in 2009!) In general, the working assumption that cultural differences are sustained in the medium term seems to be reasonable.

We are experiencing extraordinary economic change at the present time. Society as a whole is affected and this, in turn, reacts back on the economy. It is important to examine the nature of this mechanism, or 'feedback loop'. There is little doubt that sustained economic performance can improve society in several different ways. Economic growth does not have to lead to materialism or Wildean cynicism. What it does do is increase the possibility of choice for most people and that must be applauded. In Ireland, the Celtic Tiger period may also have helped the peace process in imperceptible ways. In less than a decade, the Republic of Ireland became one of the world's leading economies and was praised far and wide. This may well have fostered parity of esteem in Northern Ireland.

The Celtic Tiger period may have ended in 2001, but the melody lingered on until 2008 when we went into an unprecedented recession and the Irish banking system suffered a meltdown. The government started out by telling people not to talk down the economy, but when they wanted to cajole the unions into pay cuts in the run-up to the 2010 budget, they led the charge with pessimistic outbursts. People were confused and frightened by this sudden change in the tone of official statements. Not only was confidence lost in a matter of weeks but fear came to the surface.

There is talk about Ireland having to go to the IMF, or at least getting financial support from the stronger members of the Economic and Monetary Union (EMU), in addition to the liquidity the banks will get from the European Central Bank (ECB). Some people believe that Ireland has suffered so much reputational damage abroad that we may not be able to borrow on international capital markets, or that the costs of borrowing could become prohibitive, as they have in the case of Greece. There is even a hint of paranoia, in the sense that foreign rating agencies and market participants (who were jealous of the Celtic Tiger) have vindictively marked us down.

The government is performing disastrously in opinion polls and it is unlikely that the opposition parties would even want to form a government, so deep is the recession. People are crying out for leadership, but after eighteen months of ad hoc crisis management the government has not yet produced a comprehensive strategic plan, and it is unlikely that one will be forthcoming.

The first budget of 2009 unravelled, the social partners failed to reach an agreement, recapitalisation of the main banks has not impressed the capital markets, and we have had demonstrations in the streets, especially in the run-up to the 2010 budget. Taxpayers have been put on the hazard by the creation of the National Asset Management Agency (Nama) which will overpay the banks for their property-related loans. If the overpayment is not large enough, the government will have to inject even more capital into the banks. While estimates vary wildly, it is likely that taxpayers will ultimately have to pay a huge bill of over €30 billion, including the money injected into Anglo Irish Bank. Some of this might be clawed back from the banks by way of levies, but the banks have always had an uncanny ability to pass such levies on to customers who, in most cases, are also taxpayers. Ironically, it is by no means certain that any of these costly and convoluted measures will get the banks to lend to small businesses again. In 2010 it was clear that many businesses were still going to the wall; thus, productive capacity was being steadily lost.

While the two budgets of 2009 focused mainly on increased taxation, the budget of 2010 concentrated on cuts in public sector pay and social welfare. This also involved the collapse of the pay talks and quite possibly the end of social partnership. The budget for 2011 will also seek to take another €3–4 billion out of the economy, and the adjustment will not end there. Unemployment has shot up to over 453,000 and living standards and wealth have plummeted. The wrench from the quilted days of the Celtic Tiger to the harsh realities of today has been extraordinary and could have an undermining effect on the national psyche. Will we be able to cope?

The government has tried to blame this unfortunate turn of events on external factors, such as the collapse of Lehman Brothers. But a report by the new Governor of the Central Bank, Professor Patrick Honohan, does not accept that, and argues that the government was instrumental in overheating the economy, fuelling the property bubble, and ignoring the fragilities of the tax base. Unless we admit our own responsibility for recession and bank failures, it will be difficult to rectify the situation. We did make serious mistakes and it is important to set out the main ones and try to learn from them. During the good years we should have:

- Recognised that devaluation was not an option in EMU and used social partnership to keep pay increases in line with those in European Union member states (that is, 2 per cent a year, instead of the actual 4.5 per cent a year) and thus safe-guarded competitiveness

- Planned for a less favourable configuration of exchange rates

- Kept government spending on a moderate growth path, knowing that windfall property-related taxes would not continue indefinitely

- Widened the tax base

- Put more of our windfall revenue into the National Pension Reserve Fund

- Finished road and rail projects, thus bringing infrastructure up to speed

- Ensured that public expenditure achieved value for money

- Used cost-benefit analysis for this purpose

- Put more resources into research and development

- Intervened in the property market to prevent a bubble

- Recognised the 'pyramid' scheme aspects of the property market and the huge dependence on construction and re-lated activity

- Recognised the fact that consumer spending was based so much on borrowing that it could not continue

- Used our regulatory system and the Central Bank to moderate the behaviour of the banks

- Formulated an industrial strategy, with less dependence on foreign multinationals.

Unfortunately, none of these things was done. The government decided to listen to the cheerleaders and not the warning voices. It was as if the government believed that everyone woke up on the morning of New Year's Day 1995 (the birth of the Celtic Tiger) and suddenly became more dynamic and entrepreneurial. They did not understand that cultural change, if and when it occurs, is an extremely slow process.

Members of government frequently alluded to their role in creating the Celtic Tiger. No one asked them what they had done to perform such a miracle. They had of course done nothing. The 'miracle' was the result of a critical mass of US foreign direct investment and the influence of much lower interest rates following Ireland's EMU membership. But instead of recognising that it was largely the result of a fluke of history, we engaged in hubris. It was not the first time this has happened and it won't be the last, but we should be aware of our propensity to lurch from mania to depression.

Correcting the public finances is a painful process and various groups have been hit. There is a widespread belief that the pain is not being shared equally and this has brought people on to the streets. Social welfare payments and public sector pay had been quite generous in Ireland, and probably needed to be trimmed back in the 2010 budget, but, unfortunately, the belief that these cut-backs were to bail out wealthy bankers has created a divisive and hostile environment. As well as anger and fear, there is also a profound sense of shock. Few people believe that the government can provide leadership. Unfortunately, these negative sentiments will make economic recovery more difficult.

Many people cannot believe that bankers behaved so badly and that the financial regulator did so little. To take but one example, it came to light that Anglo Irish Bank had lent up to €500 million to each of fifteen property developers. This must have been known by the regulator, and by the government, yet nothing was done. The other banks followed Anglo blindly in a downward spiral, a classic race to the bottom.

The conceptual framework that underlay the economies of the Western world may be in the process of revision.[6] The market 'model' clearly failed yet again where banks and property were concerned. Governments in the West are now controlling the wages of bankers and bringing in tougher forms of regulation which would outlaw certain financial products. This is a form of *dirigisme* which would have been unthinkable as recently as early 2008. Maybe the market model will make a comeback, but maybe not. No one knows what might replace it. This is another cause of uncertainty.

The danger for Ireland is that economic unrest might turn into a nightmare of strikes and other forms of civil disturbance. The Croke Park agreement on public sector pay may or may not defuse this risk. Irish people are reluctant to accept 'necessary adjustments'; it is not just a matter of money, but also of pride and self-respect. Anyone who believes that economics is about technical relationships rather than people should look to Ireland at the present time.

The basic question posed by this book has been thrown into stark relief by the recession and the banking collapse: Have Irish people got the inner resources to cope with the crisis and develop the economy in subsequent years?

1

THE HUMAN FACTORS
OF PRODUCTION

'Think how hard physics would be if particles could think' – Murray Gell-Mann, *The Quark and the Jaguar*

The contention of this chapter is that all the traditional factors of production are essentially human in nature, in the sense that they can be exploited only by people. How we use the factors of production determines the long-run growth of the economy. There may be short-run blips, where, for example, consumer spending falls short of what the economy is capable of producing. But, in the long run, it is the capacity to produce goods and services that matters. That capacity depends on people in different walks of life.

Nowadays there is little discussion of the factors of production. This is because for most people and institutions – banks, stockbrokers, governments – what counts is the next year or two, so in a way nearly everyone takes a short-run view of things, which is not very healthy. Fortunately, the Economic and Social Research Institute (ESRI) does do a five-year set of forecasts, but, alas, these are discussed for a week or so and then forgotten. The media goes back to discussing last month's inflation and retail sales figures, which are important, but tell us nothing about the real prospects for the economy over the longer term.

As every school child knows, the factors of production are land and natural resources, labour, entrepreneurship and capital, which includes technology. Some countries are blessed with natural resources – gold, silver, titanium, uranium, zinc and so on – but it does not necessarily follow that these countries are guaranteed a rapid rate of economic growth. Much depends on how people manage these resources.

In Ireland, for example, we may not be overendowed with minerals, but we have fertile land and high rainfall which means that cattle can be reared quite easily and cheaply. We also have a large coastline and abundant fish stocks, at least we had until recently. How have we managed these natural resources?

In the early years of Ireland's membership of the EEC, large sections of our fishing grounds were negotiated away because at the time they were not being utilised very much. The fishing industry in Ireland is now in a very poor state. The same is true of agriculture. EU policies have not helped to exploit our natural resources on behalf of the Irish people. The important point to note here is that the physical existence of natural resources is not enough; they must be properly managed by the country's citizens and government. Certainly in the early years of the EEC, Irish farmers did well from grants, subsidies and guaranteed prices, but they were sowing the seeds of problems further down the road.

Ireland seems to be well endowed with renewable sources of energy – wind, wave and tides. To date, however, there has been little development of these resources, with one or two notable exceptions. In the 1970s the Irish government gave excessively generous terms to foreign oil and gas exploration companies. The same is broadly true regarding the gas find, currently being exploited by Shell off the west coast of Ireland. These are examples of how the human factor failed in the exploitation of natural resources.

Labour is an important factor in every country. For many years in Ireland we had a high unemployment rate, and a high rate of emigration. Each person lucky enough to have a job had to support more dependants, whether young or old, than was typical in other EU countries. During the Celtic Tiger years all that changed, and our dependency rate fell to normal levels. Moreover, greater access to secondary and tertiary education meant that there were more people available to work in high-tech US multinationals. Work is a human activity and our attitudes towards work, and the role of trade unions and social partnership, are all determined by human behaviour. Perhaps social partnership was deemed necessary in Ireland to curb a national subversive attitude towards hierarchical relationships – a tendency that can and should be allowed free rein in other fields, such as the arts.

Entrepreneurship is, of course, a human quality that can be subdivided into innovation, risk-taking and the work ethic. It will be argued later that entrepreneurship is also culture-specific, although, because of globalisation, there is now a degree of Americanisation in the enterprise models of most countries. Enterprise depends to some degree on education and special training, but it is not entirely clear whether entrepreneurship itself can be taught.[1]

It has been argued with some justification that this is by far the most important factor of production because it is the entrepreneurs who harness all the other factors. They employ workers, for example, and exploit land and natural resources. (Farmers are entrepreneurs as well as workers, except where gentlemen farmers are concerned!) Entrepreneurs formulate business plans, consult with workers, invest in their businesses and hence build up the capital stock. They ensure that the latest technology is embodied in the capital they are using. They also have to ensure that the factors are being used in the best proportions and that profits are maximised over time. It also falls to them to decide whether or not to go public, that is, to issue shares and thereby dilute their own control. Moreover, they have to decide whether or not to break into export markets and how best to do so.

In fact, most of the important decisions in an economy are taken by entrepreneurs. In 2008/09 the financial entrepreneurs in the US and other countries, including Ireland, racked up extraordinary failures. They had no vision and followed the property bubble blindly. New financial products, especially securitised sub-prime mortgages and hedge funds, multiplied the difficulties. While bank regulation also failed dismally, it is the financial entrepreneurs, who paid themselves millions of dollars a year, who were shown to be grossly incompetent – to such an extent that they threatened the economic stability not just of the US but of the developed world. Entrepreneurship, because it combines and harnesses all the other factors of production, is the major force for good or ill. It is most definitely a human factor; one might say all too human.

To the extent that entrepreneurs may lack integrity, most countries, even capitalist ones, regulate various forms of economic activity. Individual self-interest does not always lead to the common good, and governments have to know when and how to regulate the private sector.

Capital appears to be a technical factor of production but it is not. It is savers who accumulate the money, bankers who lend it, and entrepreneurs and other investors who turn the money into capital goods, such as factories, plant and equipment, office buildings and so on. The investment done each year adds to the existing capital stock. Some countries invest a lot each year as a percentage of Gross Domestic Product (GDP) while others do not. Governments invest mainly in infrastructure, and many of these projects are quite large. Nevertheless, in Western countries private sector entrepreneurs are the largest investors and they play a very important role.

Nowadays it is not so much the quantity of the investment that counts as much as the quality.[2] If the investment 'embodies' the latest thinking and research, it will tend to be more productive than the more traditional 'picks and shovels' variety. This is another reason why capital is not a technical factor. Its quality and productivity depend crucially on human abilities in research and technological innovation.

In fact, human capital is more important than physical capital in today's world. This is especially true in countries that have transformed themselves into information economies. It is no coincidence that Bill Gates is the richest man in the world or that Silicon Valley is the engine of US economic growth. The revolution that brought us the information (or knowledge) economy reinforces the notion that it is human beings of talent, skill and education who fundamentally determine the growth of modern economies. They may implement their knowledge themselves by forming their own companies, or they may sell their ideas to existing entrepreneurs.

An important question discussed later is whether or not Ireland has had growth too easy. Our dependence on foreign direct investment (FDI), especially from the US, is unique. This investment already contains the fruits of American research and development, technology, management experience, readymade markets and other forms of know-how. The fact that this substantial and valuable investment is grafted on to the Irish economy and does not come from 'within' raises questions about our indigenous capacity for growth and development. Certainly, most other developed countries have had much more 'organic' internal growth processes than Ireland.

We are fortunate that the information economy does not require experience in old-style assembly-line systems, because, for historical reasons, we have little experience of those systems, but the lack of a tradition in old-fashioned industrial skills does not seem to be a handicap where information technology is concerned. We have essentially leap-frogged from agriculture into the information economy without having gone through the industrial phase. As Fintan O'Toole puts it, we have gone from pre-modernity to post-modernity in one jump.[3] This may well be a unique pattern of development but it does not seem to have serious drawbacks. Indeed, it may be better not to have the 'industrial baggage' or the entrenched class system that went with the nineteenth-century 'mill-owning' era. On the other hand, there may be some disadvantages, such as complacency and difficulty dealing with hierarchies.

In the early years of our economic take-off, in the 1960s, some multinational industries set up in Ireland. In several cases they employed people from farming areas. Many people found it difficult to stay in the factory environment for the requisite number of hours every day, and there were stories of workers bunking off to help with the harvest. Indeed, in the Irish civil service there were special-leave provisions right up to the 1970s to allow people to help with the harvest. Nevertheless, the development of the IT phase seems to have occurred without any friction. In fact, casual observation suggests that Irish people below a certain age like working with computers, and they enjoy the informal atmosphere and casual dress code of knowledge-based companies. They regard this kind of work as 'cool'.

A relatively high standard of education is important for the reasons mentioned above. However, the failure rate in mathematics at second-level is worrying, as is the growing evidence of grade inflation and rote learning. It must be remembered that it is no longer enough to monitor and copy existing technologies; we must be in the forefront of research and innovation. We need to focus on post-doctoral levels of education in mathematics and science. Since Asian peoples, for example, seem to have special aptitudes for these subjects, we have to take every opportunity to keep standards as high as possible in order to compete.

Enough has been said to indicate that whatever factor of production we are talking about – land, natural resources, labour, entrepreneurship, capital and technology – it is people who manage these resources and bring them to life. The Japanese have one way of doing it; the Irish have another way.

I once asked a friend from Haiti why his country had not developed. He reminded me that Haiti was the first country to experience a successful slave revolt. He asked me what I thought newly freed slaves would most desire. I gave a few answers, including 'money' and 'goods and services'. He shook his head. 'What they most wanted,' he said, 'was leisure'. In his view, it was the dreadful social and historical legacy which had inhibited development.

In Ireland it has long been argued that we have not been too generously endowed with natural resources and that, as a result, the development of the economy depended to an even greater extent on our people. There is a lot of truth in this – assuming of course that people are committed to development and all it involves.

The US is blessed with abundant natural resources, but perhaps an even greater strength is the attitude of Americans to technology. For a long while in Europe, scientists and academics believed that applying science to practical problems was somehow beneath their dignity. This was never a consideration in the US where the application of science to create many different technologies was actively encouraged. Indeed, over the years, many top European scientists were attracted to the US by the much higher remuneration available to skilled people who were prepared to work in technology. A high social standing was, no doubt, an additional incentive.

Enough has been said to illustrate that it is people who organise and run economies – entrepreneurs, investors, educators, consumers, workers, public officials and politicians. The so-called factors of production would not be worth much without people power. The performance of economies depends critically on people and on their culture-induced behaviour. How economies react to external shocks or to changes in policy will also depend on these behaviours.

2

COMPONENTS OF THE PEOPLE ECONOMY

'Apart from the known and the unknown what else is there?' – Harold Pinter, *The Homecoming*

We have seen how 'economic agents' – that is, people – manage the factors of production and how this determines the long-term growth path or pace of development. It was also noted that in the short run an economy may not grow at full capacity. Perhaps governments raise taxes too much and consumer demand slows down. If this happens, then unsold goods remain on the shelves and the message filters back to producers, who decide that they should reduce production for the time being. This is essentially what is meant by a growth recession – that is, the economy is growing below its capacity for a while, usually no longer than a year or two. Sooner or later, though, the economy in question tends to get back to its longer-term capacity growth path, unemployed workers are re-employed and standards of living rise. It is not being suggested, however, that the recession in Ireland will be so easily corrected.

The so-called Keynesian revolution' postulated that governments could expand demand by increasing its own spending or lowering taxes, and thereby minimising, or even preventing, recessions. The idea was that if an economy could grow smoothly without stops and starts, entrepreneurs would become more confident about the long-term future and invest in productive capacity more than they otherwise would.

Imagine the factors of production being the engine of a car and the people who mobilise them being the driver. It may be a strong car or a weak one, but the journey will be below potential if there are potholes in the road. If the latter can be fixed by government, then the car will perform better and the driver will have more confidence.

It is advisable to set out the structure of a typical economy in order to show exactly how and where people make their contributions to growth. This structure is based on the national accounts and is adopted by virtually every country in the world.[2]

There are three ways of viewing (and measuring) Gross Domestic Production (GDP) – expenditure, incomes and output.[3] Sometimes expenditure is called 'the demand side' and output is called the 'supply side'. Remember President Reagan's supply-side economics? He favoured this side because it tends to be dominated by private sector producers and big corporations. He de-emphasised the demand side because that was where government tends to exercise its influence, as we shall see later. Reagan (and Margaret Thatcher) wanted to reduce the role of government in the economy because, according to their ideologies, government could never be as efficient as the private sector. The supply-siders also favoured low taxes, partly because this would prevent governments from meddling too much in the economy, and partly because lower taxes would incentivise private entrepreneurs and workers.

The next thing to note is that GDP should be exactly the same whichever of the three sides it is measured from. Whether or not it turns out to be equal in practice is a moot point and one that we will gladly leave to the black arts of national accountants and central statistics offices around the world. These necromancers have ways of making the three measures equal! In any case, GDP is usually taken to be the best measure of a country's economic welfare. It shows how much the country has produced in a year (or a quarter), how much it has spent and how much income it has earned. The concept of 'national income' is much the same as GDP. Clearly, if these items grow rapidly, then so will living standards. If we have 'good' factors of production (see Chapter 1), then there is every chance that living standards or GDP will grow and develop at a satisfactory pace and add to the 'wealth' of the country concerned.

Table 1: The Basic Structure of Every Economy

Expenditure	Income	Output
Consumption	Wages	Manufacturing
Investment	Profit	Construction
Government		Agriculture
Exports		Services
–Imports		
GDP =	GDP =	GDP

Note: For the sake of simplicity, some small, technical items are omitted. In 2009 the value of GDP in Ireland was around €200 billion or €45,000 per head of population, which placed Ireland in the top five countries in the world. The GNP measure is somewhat lower. GDP is the same whether it is 'added up' from the expenditure, income or output sides, hence the equality signs in the last row of Table 1.

The three sides of any economy influence each other every minute of every day. They depend on each other. For example, people have to earn income in order to consume goods and services; and the only way they can earn income is by producing or helping to produce goods and services. In turn, workers and entrepreneurs who generate the output will do so only if there is a demand for it. Which comes first, expenditure, income or output? It is like the chicken and the egg. This loop operates in every economy in the world, and it is known as the 'circular flow of income'.

The factors of production that we looked at earlier feed primarily into the output (supply) side. Entrepreneurship, labour, natural resources, capital and technology largely determine how much output can be produced in any given year. More correctly, it is the human motivations and skills behind these factors of production which determine output.

At one stage in the history of economic thought it was believed that supply (or output) created its own demand (or expenditure). As noted earlier, John Maynard Keynes thought this was not necessarily true, and that in the short term demand could be deficient, with the result that people could become unemployed. In such situations he recommended that governments provide a stimulus to boost demand. We shall see later if this is still the great idea it once was.

Another way of stimulating an economy is if the central bank reduces interest rates. This should encourage entrepreneurs to borrow more money to invest in plant and equipment. Both the expenditure side and the output side would be boosted. The lower interest rates might also encourage consumers to take their money out of banks and spend more on goods and services. They might also be encouraged to take out mortgages to buy houses. It is difficult to know whether a house is an investment good or a consumer good, but the national accounting convention is to put house construction in under 'investment' and, naturally, it will also appear on the output side of the accounts under 'construction'.

If the government and/or central bank overstimulate the economy – via fiscal and/or monetary policy – a situation can develop where the demand side begins to outstrip the output side. But the two sides must remain equal, so what is it that maintains the equality if consumers spend a lot and producers cannot keep up? The answer is prices. Inflation will increase to maintain the equality in current price terms. And the trouble with inflation is that it is another big pothole in the road that makes people uncertain about the future and tends to reduce the confidence needed for a steady stream of investment and growth.

GDP, and indeed all the national accounts headings, measure what is called *final* demand or *final* output. Thus, the timber and cement used as inputs in houses, say, will not appear as separate outputs, only the final value of the house. By the same token, social welfare payments by government to various people will not appear as such because these payments will already have been 'consumed' or 'invested'. In fact, on the expenditure side of the accounts, the 'government' item simply measures what the government itself consumes, for example the services of public officials. The government's spending on infrastructure and other capital items appears along with private sector investment under the 'investment' heading.

Many people are confused by the difference between the money supply and GDP (or national income). Indeed, some people believe that the money supply is the same as GDP, but it is not. Think of GDP as the sum total of final output (of buckets and computers and haircuts and so on, which are all magically added together by brilliant statisticians). It has nothing to do with money, which people keep in the bank or post office. But every time we go into a shop to buy a bucket or computer, we have to pay with money. Money is the oil that lubricates the millions of transactions that go on every day. But it does not form part of GDP. In most countries the money supply is usually much lower than the value of GDP. In Ireland it used to be only about half. This means that it circulated twice during the year in question as it lubricated the wheels of exchange. If it circulates faster than normal, it may generate inflation, even though interest rates stay the same.

The old saying that 'inflation is caused by too much money chasing too few goods' is broadly correct. If money grows excessively, that means that people are going to use that part of it which they do not want to save for spending on goods and services. If the output of the latter is fixed in the short term, then prices will be driven up. It is just like being at an auction where there are a lot of buyers with plenty of cash and where the items for sale are in short supply; the prices can reach quite high, even ridiculous, levels. On one occasion I attended an auction where two ladies got involved in a bidding war over a few life vests. The price went way above the retail value of such items and kept on going up. Unusually, the auctioneer stopped the proceedings and had a 'time out'. He started the bidding again and the final price reached the second time was much more realistic. I had seen a classic example of overshooting. I had also witnessed an auctioneer who played the role of regulator in an enlightened way. Not all auctioneers are like this. And not all regulators are like that auctioneer!

It was noted earlier that the factors of production feed into the output side, and they have also been described as the engine of the car. Why don't we hear more about them on television and in the newspapers? We might hear occasionally about a gas discovery or about a new piece of science or technology being developed in a university somewhere, but most economic news refers to much more short-term indicators, such as retail sales or the monthly figure for inflation, or the latest estimates of government revenue. The reason for this media concentration on the expenditure (demand) side is simply because we have better and more frequent data to talk about on that side of the national accounts. But this should not be taken to mean that the expenditure side is more important that the output side. That would be like saying that the egg was more important than the chicken. Yet commentators do tend to make the assumption that if the leading indicators suggest that the expenditure side is growing quickly, then the other sides will follow suit and therefore the economy as a whole will also grow fast. This is usually a reasonable assumption but there can be occasions when the output side is suffering from bottlenecks and capacity constraints and cannot produce the goods required. At such times the economy may not grow; instead, we might see inflation increasing or we may see imports growing to fill the gap.

It is useful to go through Table 1 item by item. Every day as we read our newspapers, we see references to retail sales or housing starts or tourism receipts or government revenue. Where do all these things fit in and how do they fit together to make up an economy? Table 1 can be used to illustrate this, and also to indicate how the government can manipulate the economy by influencing the people who operate in the different sectors.

Consumption, the first item on the expenditure side, refers to all the goods and services people buy during the year (or quarter) in question. It is a very large item, which normally accounts for over 50 per cent of GDP. It is important for forecasters to get it right, so they regularly discuss retail sales and other indicators that come out on a monthly or quarterly basis. Government receipts of VAT payments are also a good indicator of how consumption is progressing. When the Celtic Tiger came to an end in 2001, consumer spending kept the economy going for another few years, but it was fed by borrowing.

Consumption is also important because it can be influenced by government in the short term. Lower taxes, for example, will usually have the effect of encouraging people to go out and spend their windfall gains. In Ireland, though, a high proportion of consumer goods are imported and this means that any boost to consumption may not have a strong 'multiplier' effect on the rest of the economy. Note that *imports*, farther down the expenditure column, has a negative sign. Increased imports will reduce GDP.

Investment, the second item, is also important, though it usually accounts for only about 20 per cent of GDP. It includes investment in plant, equipment, office and residential buildings, whether this investment is undertaken by foreign or Irish companies or by the government. It does not include investment in stocks and shares since that kind of financial investment does not go directly into the real kinds of activities listed above. What we are concerned with here is the creation of new investment assets, not transactions in existing ones.

So this kind of real investment is basically the seed-corn of the economy. In part, it reflects the decisions of a society not to consume all its GDP but to put some proportion of it aside for the future. Most investment decisions are taken by entrepreneurs. Some of them may indeed restrict their own consumption, but most entrepreneurs will borrow the money from banks or take it from retained profits. A fairly high investment-to-GDP ratio of 20 per cent or above is usually required to keep the economy growing at a reasonable rate; it is also important that the investments use up-to-date technologies. The government can influence this item directly by changing the size of the public capital programme. Investment is usually influenced

by interest rate changes as well, and by the growth of the economy. If interest rates are high and the economy is fairly sluggish,
then entrepreneurs will not be encouraged to invest.

Particular forms of investment can be promoted by special
government incentives. For example, over the past ten years or
so there were several tax-based schemes to encourage investment in holiday homes, hotels and other houses in designated
areas. These schemes are usually a mistake because they distort
market signals. (We now know to our cost how mistaken those
tax breaks were.)

Government current spending refers to the day-to-day spending of government on current goods and services and the salaries of its employees. It does not include the public capital programme, which is part of the *investment* item. In the past there
were times when government deliberately increased the size of
the civil service to create more employment. The opposite may
happen in the present recession because of the need for budget
cuts. Public sector pay has already been cut.

Exports constitute a very large and important item which appears on the expenditure side of the accounts because it reflects
the spending of foreigners on our goods and services. It includes
merchandise exports and service exports – tourism, for example.
The total comes to about 80 per cent of GDP, which is very high
by international standards. It is driven mainly by multinational
companies. The government cannot influence this item very
much, though the state agencies such as the IDA and Enterprise
Ireland do have a role here. To keep exports competitive, however, the government tries to ensure that wage and other costs
do not rise too quickly.

Imports is also an important item, about 70 per cent of GDP.
We import consumer goods and services and capital (or investment) goods. If the economy is growing rapidly, this item tends

to increase quite fast. When imports are combined with exports, we can, with the addition of some other items, calculate the current balance-of-payments position. The fact that exports and imports come to 80 per cent and 70 per cent of GDP, respectively, indicates how extremely open the Irish economy is – one of the most open in the world.

Moving across to the middle column of Table 1, we see that the first item is *Wages,* which reflects the pay-bill for everyone employed. *Wages* are the return to labour in the same way that *Profits* are the return to entrepreneurship. It is important to keep a reasonable balance between wages and profits so that workers and entrepreneurs can operate in harmony. In Ireland the breakdown is usually about 60 per cent wages and 40 per cent profits – broadly in line with other countries. During the boom years in Ireland the profit share increased considerably, to the irritation of workers and trade union leaders. On the other hand, a large part of those high profits were repatriated by the multinational companies and so were not available for distribution among the Irish workforce.

The final column of Table 1 shows the main sectors of production or output. These are: *Manufacturing, Construction, Agriculture* and *Services,* and they are the sectors where people are employed as workers and entrepreneurs. The other factors of production also feed in here and are increased by new investment (which is measured in column 1). At present, agriculture is about 2 per cent of GDP, manufacturing 25 per cent, construction 11 per cent, while services now accounts for a surprising 62 per cent of GDP. The service sector can be broken down further into distribution, transport and communication, public administration and defence, and a miscellaneous category which includes banking, insurance and other financial activities.

Many economists believe that the service sector is where future growth will come from, especially in the information economy, and it is expected that this sector could grow to 70 per cent of GDP in the not too distant future. This may have implications for training and re-training the workforce. Since the 1980s, the IDA has been attracting service-type companies into this country, and Enterprise Ireland has focused on this area as well. Some observers believe that, although many different types of service can be exported nowadays, it may be unwise to base future economic growth solely on services.

Before leaving Table 1, it might be useful to mention that the overall performance of the economy (the growth in real GDP) should be assessed by reference to the individual items that are driving it. Suppose there were a few years where the main driver of growth was consumption and where investment and exports were more or less flat; we might well have cause to worry. This kind of growth composition might not be that healthy. We could be consuming the seed-corn and failing to build up markets abroad.

We also need to look at the output per head in manufacturing, construction and services. If productivity is not growing as fast as in other countries, then we may be losing competitiveness. There is also the question of inflation and fiscal and balance-of-payments deficits which need to be regularly monitored as part of the nation's fever chart. In other words, the growth of real GDP does not, on its own, tell the whole story about how an economy is performing. Incidentally, it tells us nothing about how incomes are distributed among the people.

The most important theme of this chapter is that whatever facet of the economy we look at, we are primarily involved in the analysis of *people* – as consumers, investors, public servants, exporters, importers, wage earners, entrepreneurs, manufacturers,

construction workers, farmers and workers involved in the service sector, ranging from computer programmers to pop singers,
from barbers to mathematicians, from waiters to train drivers.
Table 1 shows us where each group of people makes its contribution to the economy. It also shows the interdependencies involved. For example, if entrepreneurs are reluctant to invest in
their businesses, output will fall; so too will wages and consumption. How will employees and consumers react to this? We need
to look at the human motivations behind the 'sectors' to understand the numbers.

Ireland is a dual economy, especially where manufacturing,
services and exports are concerned. The presence of so many US
multinational companies cannot be overlooked. This large and
dynamic 'foreign' sector is not particularly influenced by Irish
culture-induced behaviour and is something of an enclave. It is
notable that the performance of the 'foreign' sector is quite different from that of the 'indigenous' sector.

Since the 1990s, the output performance of the foreign sector
has surpassed the indigenous sector by a factor of about six. The
statistics may be distorted to some extent by transfer pricing
but, nevertheless, the differences are amazing. Indeed, US companies account for over 70 per cent of our total exports.

Foreign direct investment is extremely productive. It embodies the fruits of research and development done in the US and it
comes with advanced technologies, ready-made markets and
proven business plans and know-how. This means that the benefits of this kind of investment to Ireland are much greater than
the direct job numbers might suggest. For example, multinational companies here employ 'only' about 150,000 workers, but
the indirect effects would probably multiply this number by a
factor of three or thereabouts.

It is important, however, to concentrate on the behaviour of Irish people – entrepreneurs, politicians, public officials, consumers and employees – to see what the future looks like. This is because there is no certainty that our reliance on multinationals can continue to anything like the same extent. There are several reasons for this which will be discussed later. One reason worth mentioning now relates to tax harmonisation, particularly the possibility that Northern Ireland may introduce a preferential tax regime for foreign industry. Our failure to focus on the indigenous sector in the past has made us too complacent about the economy. We have congratulated ourselves for economic performances that were largely due to US multinationals, and have rarely acknowledged the much lower productivity of domestic enterprises. These huge differences in performance persisted right through the period of the Celtic Tiger and are still in evidence. What does this mean for the future?

3

UNUSUAL FEATURES
OF THE IRISH ECONOMY

'Ireland is a poor country full of rich people.'
– G.B. Shaw, *John Bull's Other Island*

'How much did you get for the heifer at the mart?'
'What heifer?'
'The little black and white one you had in the top field.'
'What mart?'
– Conversation overheard in County Roscommon

We have seen how people make use of the factors of production and where and how they fit into the different sectors of the economy. To understand how an economy functions, we have to appreciate what motivates people and why they behave as they do in specific cultural contexts. Before looking at how orthodox or otherwise Ireland's economic behaviour is, it is advisable to set out some of the unusual features of the economy. The structure of the Irish economy is atypical in several respects and it is important to discuss this. Otherwise, we might confuse structural peculiarities with behavioural quirks.

Ireland is a most unusual economy because it is small, extremely open, and it depends to a large extent on foreign companies attracted here by tax breaks. Unfortunately, as noted earlier, most economic textbooks are written by Americans who come from an extremely large, relatively closed economy where most of the important firms are domestically owned. Consequently, we have to be careful about applying 'American' theory to our very different structure.

Whereas Ireland used to depend too much on Britain, it is now far better diversified geographically. While the Berlin connection is important, the Boston one is much more so. This has been our secret weapon. The debate before both referenda on the Lisbon Treaty suggested that Ireland owed its good economic performance to the European Union. Not so. The American connection is far more important, though, admittedly, many US companies have set up here in order to sell into the EU. Britain is now quite a way down the list. Nevertheless, the often fraught historical relationship with the United Kingdom continues to influence our attitudes in subtle ways.

Membership of the European Monetary Union means that we have no control over interest rates or the exchange rate. Consequently, independent monetary policy is virtually non-existent. The EU also imposes rules on the conduct of fiscal policy and may in time encroach into the field of tax harmonisation. Because of the openness of the Irish economy, the effects of fiscal policy are quite limited in any case. For example, if the government tries to stimulate the economy by reducing taxes, say, a large part of the increased disposable income would be spent on imports. Part of the windfall might even be saved.

The strange institution of social partnership also reduces the government's autonomy regarding fiscal policy and pay policy. Consequently, there isn't a great deal any Irish government can do to influence the economy. There is probably no other government in the world with such limited influence on its own economy. Surprisingly, none of the main political parties in Ireland seems to regret this lack of influence or erosion of sovereignty. It is also surprising that politicians and senior public officials are so well paid by international standards when they have far fewer important decisions to make!

There seems to be a large gap between who we are as a people and the standard concept of Economic Man or Woman, whose rationality is very narrowly defined and is assumed to be the same in all cultures. Economists tend to ignore the wider cultural issues partly because they are extremely difficult to measure, let alone model. Some attempts in the past to develop a holistic approach were brave, but not quite successful.[1] Failure to predict or understand the recession and financial crisis of 2008/09 can be attributed to this partial and compartmentalised approach to economic life.

The prevailing economic model in use today does not allow for the rich complexity of human life. It is a powerful and extremely elegant model ('competitive price equilibrium') and one that is capable of refinement and development. But it can be inadequate. Some academic economists are attempting to make its assumptions more realistic,[2] but to date there is no sign of an alternative model taking over. It could well be that the subject matter of economic life is just too complex to be codified in any more meaningful way.

Those who think that economic behaviour is a culture-free zone would do well to compare the Swedish and the US economies. Both are developed Western economies, but the revealed preferences of both countries are completely different. The degree of inequality in Sweden is substantially below that in the United States. The reason for this is solely attributable to cultural differences. Swedish people are not comfortable with an economy that treats less talented people as second-class citizens. The fact that rewards for senior executives in Sweden are much less than those in the US does not lessen their work effort. The pace of development of the Swedish economy has been on a par with that of the US for a long number of years. But if the egalitarian Swedish system were imposed on the US, it probably would seriously de-motivate corporate leaders there. Why? Because the culture is different. Americans need substantial monetary incentives; Swedes do not. The economic system – capitalist or egalitarian – follows the culture, not the other way around. Strong leaders like Gorbachev or Thatcher can temporarily change the economic system, but not the fundamental culture underlying it. In the United States, President Obama clearly wants to nudge the economic system more towards equality, including the provision of health care; only time will tell whether or not he will be able to overcome cultural resistance.

Even in countries where there is a roughly similar development ethos, the means of pursuing economic goals can be very different. For example, the development processes in Japan and China continue to be quite different, with Japan favouring huge corporations and China preferring smaller businesses which tend to retain family control and labour forces which are personally selected by members of the family.[3]

The World Bank and the IMF have made mistakes in African countries partly because they did not understand the ramifications of different tribal cultures and took an excessively narrow technical approach to economic development. Fortunately, the human factor is at last being given some attention. In those countries where corruption is rife, it is very difficult to get economic development going because the single most important quality required for any economic transaction is trust, a quality that cannot be measured.

In many disciplines, assumptions have to be made where human motivations are concerned. For example, lawyers and judges find it useful to have a concept of the 'reasonable person' – or sometimes the 'right-thinking person'. Psychologists and psychiatrists use the benchmark of the 'normal' person. In the same way, economists base their theories on the 'rational' person, where rationality is defined fairly narrowly – as a desire to maximise personal welfare in all circumstances, regardless of its effects on other people. In practical terms, this means maximising personal real income. An ancillary assumption is that if everyone acts in their own self-interest, then, *à la* Gordon Gekko, the common good will be served.[4] This, however, is not what the much-maligned Adam Smith actually said. In fact, he usually qualified the term 'self-interest' with the adjective 'enlightened', and indeed his work in economics was meant to be read in the context of his earlier work on moral philosophy.[5] It is doubtful if he would ever have subscribed to the notion that greed was good. I am not sure that market economists would subscribe to this notion either.

Despite the assumptions of orthodox economics, it is unlikely that consumers are motivated solely by self-interest. Various psychological tests have shown that they are also influenced by some notion of the common good and by a sense of loyalty. Similarly, entrepreneurs are not exclusively driven by maximising profit. They also have a sense of community and often target market share and corporate growth, rather than profit per se.

In almost every economic transaction, there is a certain amount of stress, usually caused by uncertainty regarding the outcome of the transaction in question. For example, consumers may wonder whether or not the new dishwasher or meal in an up-scale restaurant will really be worth the money. Hence people tend to put a higher value on familiar products. The devil you know is better than the devil you don't. Ask anyone who has traded in a car for a second-hand model which does not have a guarantee. These concepts of fear, uncertainty and mistrust are apparently hard-wired into us and date almost from the beginnings of humankind. Proponents of the new economics regard these evolutionary responses as important for a proper understanding of economic activity. To these evolutionary impulses must be added culture-induced attitudes.

To be fair, economists do not fully rule out 'irrational' or eccentric behaviour. They argue that when dealing with large numbers of people, the relatively few examples of maverick behaviour will not be significant or will be cancelled out by opposing eccentricities. The fact that economists deal with *average* behaviour has led to the well-known quip that if a man has his head in the oven and his feet in the fridge his temperature will on average be just fine. In many cases the assumption of rational average behaviour is borne out by the data. But consider the following examples, drawn mainly from Irish experience, which would hardly be consistent with the narrow rationality posited by theory.

Work is supposed to cause disutility. That is, employees get negative welfare from working. Wages are paid to compensate for this. Yet in Ireland it seems that many people (not just a few eccentrics) actually like their work, and appreciate the opportunities for socialising, networking and having a standing in the community. Those who have lost their jobs in the recession would dearly like to have them back. To have a job, many people are prepared to commute for several hours a day in bad traffic conditions and often pay expensive crèche charges. In many cases, the net income left over can be small and it is difficult to explain such decisions solely by reference to economic rationality.

It may be argued that many people need a second income, however small, to help pay off a mortgage. If that is part of the explanation, it raises another question: the Irish obsession with house ownership at almost any cost. This is surely a matter of cultural (post-colonial) legacy rather than of economic rationality. In other economies – France, Germany and Italy – much higher proportions of the population rent properties. The desire on the part of Irish people to own bricks and mortar extends beyond the family home, into second or third properties, often in foreign countries. Indeed, many Irish property speculators bought huge trophy buildings in London and New York, in several cases paying excessive prices. This modern version of 'land hunger' came close to being pathological.

In the public sector, several individuals have gone the extra mile to serve the national interest without personal compensation. How can one 'rationalise' the major contributions made by, for instance, Ken Whitaker, Roy Geary, Louden Ryan, Donogh O'Malley and Noel Browne? Unfortunately, there is much less of this particular kind of 'irrational' behaviour today. Cooperation in the workplace is also irrational. Nevertheless, it has often been observed that employees help each other, which, according to theory, they shouldn't do since they are all competing for limited promotional opportunities or for bonuses.

There are many philanthropists in Ireland who want to donate monies to universities, hospitals and churches. Many ordinary people give generously to charities or donate blood for free, while others do voluntary social work. On a per capita basis, Ireland is still one of the most generous contributors to the Third World and many commentators take the view that this has some causal connection with the Famine of the nineteenth century.

Religious people may be motivated by the promise of the Hereafter while businessmen may enjoy the publicity and bragging rights. Ireland, on its own, has a negligible effect on global warming, but we nevertheless want to play our part in costly environmental policies.

It is hard to integrate such 'unprofitable' activities into mainstream economic theory. Even the fairly recent concept of *social capital* does not quite capture them. Indeed, it is not even considered rational for a parent to wish to leave money to their children because it does not increase the parent's welfare. Feeling a warm glow does not qualify as 'welfare'. Sometimes economists try to widen the concept of welfare to include more 'psychic' aspects. Why, for example, would any businessman give money to a politician if no favours were done in exchange? Like Mr Spock, most economists would argue that such a transaction would be illogical. Nevertheless, we know that such transactions are common enough. What the businessman gets in return is a sort of psychic income or utility which can take the form of impressing his peers or simply a feeling of being close to power. It is, however, very difficult to incorporate psychic income into the national accounts, not least because of measurement difficulties.

Irish people tend not to take a long-term view of things. Survey evidence suggests that we would prefer to have €100 today than €150 next year. This is a very high rate of discounting the future. It is, understandably, higher for older people. There seems to be a strong preference for instant gratification. It could also reflect historical experiences; on many occasions in the past better futures were promised – but never came.

Since 'a week is a long time in politics', it is likely that politicians discount the future at a very high rate indeed. Probably the period beyond the next general election has no significance whatsoever! These attitudes are hardly consistent with the investment needs of a modern economy and may explain in part why we depend so much on foreign investment.

Many Irish people would prefer to get €2 back from the tax-man than to get a gift of €3 from some other source. This makes no sense in economic terms, yet the cultural pull in favour of tax avoidance (or 'sheltering', to use the latest euphemism) is strong in this country. During the troubles in Northern Ireland, it was a Catholic's duty to shelter as much tax as possible from the UK Revenue Service. No doubt, in earlier periods it was considered virtuous to skimp as much as possible on the rent paid to absentee landlords. Irish people may not be regarded as feckless nowadays, but there is little doubt that a people who suffered from unfair laws imposed by a colonial power do not always take the law at face value or regard it as having much moral force.

How many of us in Ireland make the marginal decisions that theory requires us to make? How many would change jobs for an extra €5 per week? How many would do their grocery shopping in three or four different supermarkets in order to buy the loss-leader items on offer in each store? Who among us would haggle with a lawyer or doctor over their fees? Most of us will not even send back a steak that is undercooked. We may try to increase our personal welfare from time to time, but we do not always try to maximise it.

Markets do not work as well as they are supposed to and the gap between theory and practice is very wide in Ireland. The least realistic assumption is that markets are efficient and, via competitive forces, lead to the best allocation of resources for the community. This assumption is based on extremely stringent conditions that rarely exist in practice – certainly not in Ireland.

It is also worth noting that the banking fiasco that began in 2008 is a clear example of market failure. It is amazing to hear President Obama and Brian Cowen talking about the need to cap bankers' salaries and to toughen up the regulatory environment. Three years ago such talk would have been regarded as heresy because it was believed then that unfettered markets delivered the best outcomes. If bankers were paid $5 million a year, it was because that was the wage necessary to 'clear' the market! Any wage below that would fail to attract the best people. We know better now.

The first condition for markets to work properly is that there must be perfect information. In reality this condition is not usually met. Most people do not know whether or not another bank down the street is offering better interest rates. Even if they do make the effort to find out, they will not be aware of other 'catches' in the small print. Producers and service-providers have the high ground; they can make the information as confusing as possible. Indeed, in mid-2008 we had the bizarre spectacle of estate agents publishing incorrect prices achieved for houses on their books when the market started to weaken. Perfect information is the exception rather than the norm in Ireland. Most consumer bodies advise us to 'shop around'. Unfortunately, doing that is very time-consuming and involves additional 'search' costs.

Between Pearse and Connolly railway stations in Dublin there are a number of shops that sell Polo mints. The price should, according to theory, be the same in each shop. In fact the price varies from 55 cent to 95 cent, in other words, by over 70 per cent within a square mile. Even if consumers of Polo mints were aware of these price differences, are they really going to walk an extra mile to save 40 cent?

The 'law of one price' does, however, seem to operate in Moore Street and that is because the stalls are so close together that it is easy to 'shop around'. The vendors also call out their prices – sometimes rather loudly – thus improving information.

But how many Moore Streets are there? It is a pity that banks and big corporate producers do not operate more like the ladies of Moore Street.

Producers know more about their goods and services than consumers do. This 'information asymmetry' gives the seller a distinct advantage. In recent years we have had examples of information manipulation – advertising is an example – and, unfortunately, downright deception, which is designed to 'con' consumers. It is practically impossible for the state or indeed the many regulators to ensure that information is correct.

There are also circumstances where even if we know we are being fleeced, we will agree to pay high prices. Obvious examples include matters of life and death, and helping family members in trying times. But there are less dramatic instances too, especially where a sort of tribal behaviour is involved. Sports fans are often fleeced when they travel abroad to support their teams, but they still head off to the games.

Good, reliable information is the exception rather than the norm. The main condition underlying perfect competition and efficient markets is not met in practice. In Ireland the various consumer bodies have not improved the situation very much.

The second condition is that there should be so many producers and service-providers that each has a small market share and cannot influence the market in any way. There may be some chance of this condition being met in a very large country like the United States, but in Ireland this condition does not hold, except possibly in Moore Street. While collusion has recently been outlawed here, there is nothing to stop a few top executives having an occasional phone conversation. They do not even have to meet in smoke-filled rooms. During the boom, what was to stop property developers from agreeing among themselves to withhold building land from the market?

In fact, property developers and estate agents were able to stage-manage the market – on some occasions causing potential buyers to sleep all night in queues to buy properties off the plans the next morning. In many cases, the purchasers did not even know the dimensions of the apartments they were buying. There was not enough serviced land coming on the market, which was very surprising in a sparsely populated country like Ireland. This led to panic-buying and an unsustainable surge in land prices.

We have become aware of instances where one financial institution helped another one to 'window-dress' its end-year accounts. These institutions were supposed to be in competition with each other, yet here they were colluding in a deception right under the noses of various regulatory bodies.

In short, there are not enough genuinely competitive businesses in Ireland to ensure that competitive price equilibrium is established. The second condition is not met. This, incidentally, is one of the main reasons why long-suffering Irish consumers cross the border or travel to New York to shop. It also helps explain the poor export performance of indigenous Irish companies. If a company does not compete well at home, it is unlikely to do so abroad.

The third condition is free entry – that is, anyone should be able to enter the market as a producer or service-provider. This condition may be partially met in Ireland, but there are still problems. The start-up costs may inhibit new entrants. Assuming that initial capital can be raised, a new entrant to a market might simply accept the status quo and decide not to compete. In Ireland, there is reluctance on the part of new members of a club to 'take on' the existing members. The latter might round on the 'blow-in' and use their collective power to force him out of business. He would probably acquire a reputation as a 'boat-rocker' and would not be popular in the 'right' circles. Consequently, a quiet life is generally preferred. Why do young GPs decide not to make house calls? Why do most professions charge scale fees laid down by professional associations? Why do the children of non-legal families not usually enter the legal profession? Even when there are new entrants, there are subtle ways of making them conform to the rules of the club, even if these rules are not written down.

There was the well-known case of a young GP who set up a practice in a small town. He kept his fees significantly lower than the other doctors and poached some (not many) of their patients. He was an idealist, however, and refused to hand out disability certificates to his patients unless he was absolutely convinced that they were suffering from a disability. After a few months he lost many of his patients, who went back to the more expensive but less strict doctors. The new man gradually began to conform to the standards of the profession and of the 'tribal elders'. In other words, he became a team-player – another euphemism. In the professions, peer pressure is subtle but effective. In a small country like Ireland, where tribal affiliations are strong and boat-rockers are in short supply, the free-entry condition is only partly met.

If we want evidence that free markets do not work well at an international level, we need only look to the various banking crises from 1925 to the present day. In fact, foreign-exchange markets often perform badly and display excessive volatility. Currencies can remain far removed from their fundamental values for sustained periods of time. And remember, these are deep markets with almost perfect information and thousands of participants. If *they* do not conform to the theory, no markets will. Again, even in huge international financial markets, we tend to overlook the human factor. Market participants suffer from panic and herd instincts. People do not always behave rationally, at least not in the narrow sense of economic theory.

In 2008/09 the shares of the main Irish banks collapsed from about €18 to some 15 cent! Despite the severe difficulties the banks were in, the share collapse was overdone and it is clear that stock exchange participants panicked and stampeded away from Irish equities. Stampedes cannot be stopped. You just have to wait for the frightened animals to tire themselves, or to move on to another part of the savannah.

The reason why stampedes occur is not too hard to understand. If you are a fund manager and you see that all other fund managers are selling equities, you will have a strong incentive to join them, even if you believe the equities are undervalued. Why would you not have the courage of your convictions and start buying the shares? Because if you go against the herd and get it wrong, then you will lose your job. If, on the other hand, you keep with the herd and you *all* get it wrong, you will not lose your job because everybody else would have to be sacked as well. There *is* safety in numbers. That is why we get extreme volatility in certain asset prices.

But, in theory, this shouldn't happen. Consider the following story. A Harvard Professor of Economics is walking with a student in a quad when the student spots a $20 bill in a flowerbed. He points it out to the Professor, who becomes irritated and says that, according to the rules of arbitrage, there can be no risk-free profit; therefore the $20 bill cannot exist. The student apologises for his momentary hallucination and both of them walk on. A gardener waits until they pass, then rushes forward and quickly pockets the $20 bill. Sometimes theory is too smart for its own good. In truth, theory is important for the development of the discipline but as a means of analysing the here and now it has drawbacks.

An economist once argued that if Ireland stopped American troops using Shannon airport there would be no question of the US withdrawing any investment from Ireland. This was because private sector firms were motivated only by profit and, since the low tax regime would still be in place, the US firms would stay. Theoretically, this argument was correct – but look at the practical issues that were omitted. First, it is not just the low tax rate that attracts American industry to Ireland; it is also the double taxation treaties which are co-signed by the US government. Many of these tax treaties could be revoked at the stroke of a pen. Second, if the US government wanted to teach Ireland a lesson by urging some of its own private sector companies to pull out, it probably would not require a great deal of persuasion, since many of these companies depend on US government contracts and goodwill. Again, the economic argument, though technically correct, was just too narrowly based.

Another example close to home was the case of Irish Ferries, which in 2007 tried to substitute cheaper foreign labour for its existing labour force. Most economists saw nothing wrong with that – it conformed with the theory of profit maximisation – but the Irish community and government did not want it to happen. This particular application of economic theory was not considered fair, and Irish people have a strong sense of fairness. At the present time the required fiscal adjustments are being challenged by many people on the grounds of fairness.

In government circles the property boom in Ireland was largely assumed away in the belief that the market was working efficiently according to the dictates of economic theory. The Department of the Environment told the IMF in late 2007 that there was no property bubble in Ireland and that the market was working well.[6] We also know that the Minister for Finance refused to intervene in the market because he believed it to be working efficiently. To realise that there was a serious property bubble, all one had to do was visit a 55 square metre one-bedroom apartment in an ordinary location on the north side of Dublin which had sold for €350,000. There was no need for close analysis to recognise the bubble; it filled the tiny, biscuit-tin flat from wall to wall.

In general, Irish people are down to earth and equipped with common sense. Yet there were aspects of the Celtic Tiger period, and particularly the property boom, that caused many of us to lose a sense of reality. No doubt part of this was caused by spin doctors and the feverish patois of estate agents. Maybe part of it was attributable to the fact that for once we had the opportunity of boasting about our own country. Those who did suggest that the party would stop at some stage were severely chastised. We were told that the boom would continue indefinitely. Whether all the hype was due to political opportunism, faulty technical advice or genuine self-delusion remains to be seen. The government never seemed to realise that it was encouraging people to spend and incur debt that they could not afford. Instead of trying to dilute the punch at the party, the government kept pouring in surgical spirit. Consequently, the plunge into recession and the shock to people's confidence were all the greater. It is interesting to note that in the 2010 budget speech, the Minister for Finance spoke about turning points and the worst being over. It was far too soon for such optimism. To make such comments when he was bringing in his third deflationary budget in two years was ill-advised.

Just as our political system still tends to reflect civil war politics, so our economic system mirrors our history and culture, and is charmingly idiosyncratic. Many foreign visitors who came to learn about the Celtic Tiger economy left our shores with perplexed expressions on their faces.

International bodies such as the Organisation for Economic Cooperation and Development (OECD) and the International Monetary Fund described Ireland as a market-oriented, capitalist economy. In fact, right up until the banking collapse of 2008, we were ranked next to the US and UK in this regard. Indeed, our more corporatist colleagues in the EU tend to regard us in much the same light. When we were getting ready to join the euro there was a debate at the European Central Bank about the possibility of retailers rounding up their prices as soon as the euro was adopted. During this debate, a Finnish colleague remarked that, although this might occur in other European countries, it couldn't happen in Ireland because of competition and the free play of market forces! Since Britain did not join the euro, Ireland was seen as the only standard-bearer for the free market.

I once rang the Royal Institute of Architects in Ireland. A young lady told me that the standard fee for an architect would be 12 per cent of the cost of the works. I suggested that it would be possible to negotiate that figure. 'Oh no,' she replied, 'that would not be possible at all.' I asked why not and the reply was as innocent as it was revealing: 'For goodness sake,' she said, 'that would be competition.' So much for the free play of market forces. Her tone of voice suggested that 'competition' was a dirty word like 'haggling' or 'begging', and it had no place in the professions. Was she right? Which of us offers our general practitioner €30 instead of the €45–€60 asked for?

Our proximity to Britain and our dependence on US multinationals have reinforced this perception of us as hard-nosed capitalists. And of course our experiments with privatisations (Eircom and Aer Lingus) and with private and public partnerships (PPPs) have lent credence to this view, despite the fact that many observers have grave reservations about these developments and the way some of them turned out.

To confuse matters further, the former Taoiseach, Bertie Ahern, described himself as a socialist, and some years ago imposed price controls on the pub trade. There was direct intervention in the Irish Ferries case, as has been mentioned. More recently, the state nationalised Anglo Irish Bank. Every few years we engage in a quaint exercise known as *social partnership* where wages and many other issues are decided in a centralist and totally undemocratic manner. Instead of crushing the trade unions like Mrs. Thatcher did, we love-bombed them and seduced them into the heart of the establishment where they have a sense of empowerment. The Irish approach is less confrontational and much more subtle, if not in fact devious. The sight of union leaders sweeping in and out of Government Buildings is not a comforting one, and it can cause a certain queasiness when they speak to camera and tell the citizenry to mind their own business about the negotiations. However, when social partnership was really tested in late 2009, when the 2010 budget was being prepared, the system fell apart on the issue of pay cuts in the public sector.

At one time it seemed possible that we might have found the 'third way' so keenly sought by New Labour in the UK. But that Holy Grail still eludes Western democracies and is unlikely to be found in Ireland's style of serendipity, political opportunism and residual civil war politics.

Basically, we do not conform to any known ideology and our economic system, if it is one, can only be described as pragmatic. It is as if we do not want to commit ourselves in case we box ourselves in. Less charitably, our economic system contains an element of populism or people-pleasing – a characteristic of historically oppressed nations. There may also be a vestige of the

Catholic objection to socialism – and indeed to the greed that reputedly goes with capitalism. In any event, we studiously avoid all 'isms'.

This pragmatic approach applies also to fiscal policy, which has never been based on any macroeconomic theory. Indeed, it is doubtful if in the past thirty years any serious attempt has been made to use fiscal policy to achieve macroeconomic goals.[7] Each budget has usually been little more than a bookkeeping exercise with a couple of strokes and wheezes thrown in – like bus passes and decentralisation. Between 2008 and 2010 the budgets were still bookkeeping exercises, designed to reduce the enormous borrowing requirement that resulted from the collapse of the economy. There was hardly any mention of the economic implications of reducing the deficits, even though the unemployment rate was forecast to reach a catastrophic 15 per cent.

The trouble with pragmatism is that principles do not matter. A recent example of this was our acceptance of America's use of Shannon airport during the war in Iraq. Another was the pressure put on the electorate to vote for the Lisbon Treaty in the first referendum on the grounds that if we voted against it, the rest of Europe would 'leave us behind'. Some politicians argued that a 'no' vote would make us the pariahs of Europe. It was an effective threat because in a recession we needed all the friends we could get. We also like to be liked, even though this sometimes means that we are taken for granted.

Timidity is a related characteristic which comes from our past. Despite priding ourselves on our neutrality, what have we ever used it for? Other neutral countries – Switzerland, Canada and the Scandinavian bloc – have used the goodwill that neutrality confers in a much more proactive manner. Admittedly, our diplomats and ministers for foreign affairs have been preoccupied with Northern Ireland, but it is hard to avoid the conclusion that they could have had a higher profile in international diplomacy. We have all heard of treaties and conventions linked to cities such as Geneva, Oslo and Stockholm, but there is no major international agreement associated with the name of any Irish city.

Politicians spend disproportionate amounts of time doing small favours for their constituents. The short hours spent in the Dáil give some indication of how little they do at national level. Legislation is often watered down and sometimes not even implemented. The Consumer Protection Bill, 2006 is a fairly recent case in point. Under this legislation, the National Consumer Agency (NCA) claims to be prevented from following up complaints against State agencies, even where these have monopoly power! The various finance bills are usually diluted by vested interests in the weeks following the relevant budget. Yet the propaganda and spin create the impression that the government 'runs the country'. This is not the case. Most important decisions affecting the Irish economy are now taken in Brussels, Boston and Frankfurt. And it seems as if our politicians prefer to pass decision-making to someone else, except where local clientelism is concerned. It is not an exaggeration to say that the Irish government has shrunk in importance to that of a local authority.

In the early years of EU membership senior Irish officials were timid and did not contribute much to discussions in Brussels. The large countries – Germany, France, Britain and Italy – then, as now, would have caucus meetings amongst themselves beforehand and determine the agenda for the meeting in question. If an Irish delegate did intervene to describe recent events in the Irish economy, say, the other delegates would open their newspapers and start to yawn. One way of mitigating this rudeness was to go on the attack, for example, by disagreeing with the Bundesbank's analysis of the German economy or by casting doubt on a policy paper produced by the Commission. As an attention-grabbing strategy this worked surprisingly well – the newspapers were quickly put aside – but it had to be used sparingly.

To be fair, it is hard to blame the Germans for looking askance at us. The official Irish line in those days was that Germany should become the locomotive of Europe, that is, it should lower its taxes, increase spending and thus provide a stimulus for the EU as a whole. The Irish view ignored the associated borrowing, the increase in money supply and inflation – all of which were anathema to the Germans. They must have thought we were mad – and irresponsible.

As noted earlier, in the early years of EU membership Irish farmers did well out of agricultural price supports which were primarily designed to help farmers in France and Germany. This, however, led to a belief in Irish political circles that Brussels was a 'soft touch'. By the late 1970s we had entered an embarrassing begging-bowl phase where we tried to get as much out of the Community Budget as we could. Again, the various formulae constructed by the Commission tended to favour Ireland and we began to depend on fairy money from Brussels. Before joining the currency arrangement known as the 'snake' in 1979, we pushed our luck, arguing that we needed what were then called 'resource transfers' as compensation for joining a stronger currency regime. The Germans were unimpressed and on one occasion asked a devastating question: What resource transfers had we ever received from Britain because of our link to sterling? Answer came there none!

At the time a joke did the rounds of Dublin pubs. Jack Lynch, Ireland's Taoiseach, asked the German Chancellor for eight billion Deutsche Marks. The Chancellor replied, 'Ah, Nein, Jack, Nein.' And Jack replied, 'Nine? That's even better. Thank you very much.' What happened in the end was that we got a small concessionary loan on condition that we would use it to buy German goods. In a nutshell, that is how we got the DART.

Then we embarked on major borrowing to finance our own public spending spree, and the debt dynamics began to look unstable in the early 1980s. It was suicidal to adopt lax fiscal policies precisely at a time when we had joined a strong currency regime dominated by the Deutsche Mark. (We never learned from this dreadful mistake, and repeated it after we joined the Euro in 1999.) By the early 1980s our national debt exceeded 120 per cent of GNP and the budget and balance-of-payments deficits were both in the region of 16 per cent of GNP. The soft-option approach of borrowing was coming unstuck. Our EU partners were worried about us and so was the IMF. Indeed, one of the directors of the IMF accused Ireland of hogging the available supply of international finance and thus taking bread out of the mouths of people of the Third World.

Worse was to come. Ireland was put on the IMF's 'basket-country' list in truly awful company and this shocked the Irish establishment, who knew that word would inevitably leak out – not to the press but, more importantly, to the major capitals of the world and indeed to the important banks. Our credit rating was on the line, much as it is today. If it was significantly marked down by rating agencies, Ireland would be staring bankruptcy in the face, but fortunately the shock also brought a sense of reality. In addition, many wealthy acquaintances of Irish politicians insisted that retrenchment had to be undertaken. And so it was. The late 1980s witnessed fiscal rectitude, the Tallaght Strategy and the first 'Bord Snip' which was brought into the Department of Finance to do the necessary surgery on government spending and borrowing. It was also the period when a senior politician, not known for his ascetic lifestyle, told us we were living beyond our means and needed to tighten our belts.

Then there was the embarrassing episode of 'cohesion funds' which were designed to help a less developed country like Ireland to get ready for full membership of Economic and Monetary Union. These funds were invested in infrastructure and did help the economy. Unfortunately, at this stage our European colleagues were on to us and whenever an Irish delegate would describe how well the Irish economy was doing, there would inevitably be the withering response, 'Ah, but Ireland is just a cohesion country'.

When Albert Reynolds negotiated cohesion funds of some £8 billion in 1998/99, a number of economists thought this would lead to a dependent culture and undermine whatever entrepreneurship was emerging in Ireland at the time. I attended a number of meetings where this not unreasonable argument was made. People in the audience were genuinely puzzled and thought the economists to be quite mad. Complaints were made to the organisers. It was obvious that free money was far better than earned money, wasn't it?

During the currency crisis of 1992, a crisis which was exacerbated by unguarded statements made by the then Minister for Finance, Bertie Ahern, there were rumours that the Germans were doing special interventions to support the Danish currency. The Irish government asked the Germans to do a similar 'sweetheart deal' for the Irish currency. The Germans, who objected to the term 'sweetheart deal', refused.

After the devaluation in early 1993, preparations were made for the Irish pound to enter the Eurozone. It was obvious at this stage that the Irish pound was undervalued and should be revalued before locking into the euro. But again, the Irish government wanted to go in at the existing exchange rate, with 'the wind at our backs'. The inflationary consequences were ignored and a few wiser heads suggested that there was no point in having the wind at our backs if we were heading for the rocks. In the end we revalued slightly, but only because of pressure from the Germans.

Senior policymakers were actually reluctant to join the EMU without Britain. But when Ireland did join, the volumes of foreign direct investment into Ireland rose enormously – as had been predicted. The main investor was the US which wanted to use Ireland as a platform for exporting into Europe. Ireland was the only English-speaking country in the EMU and that, despite what technical economists might say, was important to US executives – who shared Sam Goldwyn's belief that if English was good enough for Our Lord it was good enough for him. More than anything else, it was this surge of investment from the US that brought the Celtic Tiger into being. Unfortunately, the government did nothing to protect competitiveness, even though it knew that currency devaluation could never be used again.

Oddly enough, our European colleagues never fully grasped the US boost to Irish growth; they believed that Ireland had somehow pulled itself up by its own bootstraps, having had an initial kick-start from the cohesion funds. We became the poster boy of Europe, the sinner who had repented. Our own politicians took credit for the spectacular performance of the economy, which grew at over twice its historical rate. They, of course, had nothing to do with it.

The worrying thing about the Celtic Tiger is that it was yet another example of the Irish economy being improved by outside factors. Whereas previously it was agricultural subsidies, structural and cohesion funds, then huge borrowing, the Celtic Tiger boom was fuelled by top-class investment from the US which brought with it the fruits of technology and scientific research conducted in the US. Ireland did not even have to increase its spend on R&D, which, as a percentage of GNP, was, and is, one of the lowest in the OECD. In addition, the International Financial Services Centre brought in considerable investment and paid a lot of tax to the Irish government, despite the low *rate* of tax.

Although the evidence is mixed, it does not seem as if Irish firms learnt enough from these first-rate multinationals on their doorstep. While many Irish firms provided services to the multinationals, the number of new Irish companies 'spun off' from the multinationals was not as large as would have been hoped. This relative failure to emulate the foreign high-tech sector could prove to be a very serious lost opportunity. But, again, government spin-doctors will not tolerate such heresy. Instead, they claim that Ireland is well on its way to becoming an information economy – and it does not really matter if we lose low-level manufacturing jobs to India and China.

Our preferential tax regime is likely to come under pressure in the years ahead. If the large countries in the EU want more tax harmonisation, the voting modalities (including vetoes) will not stand in their way. Lawyers follow the big battalions. In addition, Barack Obama made it clear in his acceptance speech as US President that he will use the tax system to discourage American companies 'from shipping jobs overseas'. Senior British commentators have accused the Irish government of depriving the UK exchequer of tax revenue. The policy of attracting foreign direct investment has lasted for fifty years; there is no plan B.

A common thread runs through all these episodes of recent history. It is this: on no occasion did growth occur organically from within the domestic economy. In all cases the growth impetus came from abroad and was grafted on to the host economy in a rather artificial way. It was as if Ireland, like Blanche Dubois, always had to depend on the kindness of strangers. It is worrying, because it raises the question of whether we really have an indigenous growth ethos or are fatally drawn to the soft option. Since the latter can deliver impressive growth for a certain period of time, it may well mislead us and our politicians into believing that we are a growth-oriented people and that we can continue to develop under our own steam.

Self-delusion is not unknown in the political sphere. We did 'lose the run of ourselves' on other occasions. In the early 1970s, before the first oil crisis knocked us for six, there was quite a serious debate about whether or not we really should bother to promote tourism. Tourism was seen as suitable for poorer countries like Spain, but Ireland, it was argued, should aspire to something better – move up the value chain, though that expression hadn't been invented yet. Psychologists believe that feelings of inferiority and superiority can be opposite sides of the same coin.

During the Celtic Tiger years, it was all too apparent that the Irish public sector (including government) underperformed in comparison with the rest of the economy. While the private sector had the benefit of several huge foreign companies, such as Intel, Coca-Cola and Dell, the public sector was being run almost completely by Irish people. The poor performance in relation to infrastructure, health, crime and so on must have a cultural dimension. There is a tendency to be reactive rather than proactive, to cope with events as they arise rather than to engage in strategic thinking. This, of course, is consistent with our habit of discounting the future at a high rate.

Now that the economy has plunged into a deep recession, there is much hand-wringing and a danger that, in this period of poor political leadership, national confidence could suffer a serious blow.

In summary, people are motivated by several factors other than maximising their utility or welfare. These factors include self-esteem, altruism, the satisfaction of fulfilling goals, the desire to impress other people and plain old-fashioned curiosity.[8] Motivations, and their significance, vary from country to country. Thus, even the new 'behavioural economics' has to be adapted to specific cultures.

The one law of economics that is beyond reproach is that there is no free lunch, and that soft options will work only for a given period of time. There is no substitute for innovation, risk-taking and honest endeavour.

The Irish economy has several unusual features. Orthodox economic theory is sometimes not applicable to real life situations, even in capitalist countries like the United States. It seems even less applicable as an explanation of how Irish people – motivated by cultural and historical factors – go about their business.

It is important to examine more closely four categories of Irish people – entrepreneurs, public officials and politicians, consumers, and employees. There are other groupings, such as investors, importers and exporters, but these can be looked at under the heading of 'entrepreneur'.

4

HOW ENTREPRENEURIAL
ARE WE?

'We agreed that a business of his own was the only solution for him because he was obviously unemployable.'
– Peter de Vries, *Comfort Me with Apples*

'If enterprise is afoot, wealth accumulates ... and if enterprise is asleep, wealth decays.' – J.M. Keynes, *Treatise on Money*

The new 'behavioural economics' suggests that entrepreneurs are not concerned solely about price and profit. For example, firms that have monopoly power may not overcharge. This is because they belong to a wider community and are aware of the fact that their customers are concerned about fairness and can be motivated by revenge from time to time. It is interesting to note that in the United States, *the* model of liberal capitalism, the four biggest firms in several industries have 40 per cent of the market to themselves, and yet monopoly or collusive pricing does not seem to be very widespread.

I went on business to the European Central Bank in Frankfurt one October when the renowned book fair was taking place in the city. The hotel I normally stayed at had put up its prices by about 80 per cent for the five or six days of the book fair. According to the existing economics model, this was the rational thing for them to do. It was a sellers' market for that week and the hotel was simply behaving according to the law of supply and demand. But why did we all feel annoyed and exploited? One reason is that customers believe that cost, plus a mark-up, is a fair way to price and that the forces of supply and demand may not always be 'fair'. All the hotels raised their prices, even though their costs had not gone up; most customers had no option but to pay up. But we were miffed, and for the next several years a number of us avoided the main hotels in Frankfurt. In the longer term, these hotels might well have lost custom. In fact, a new hotel has recently been built which does not raise its prices during the book fair. It will be interesting to see if the newcomer will be 'persuaded' to fall into line with the opportunistic policies of other central hotels.

It is not being suggested here that entrepreneurs have to be morally superior or even likeable. The most important characteristics of entrepreneurs are dynamism, alertness, the ability to take risks and decisions, and a capacity to innovate. To require sainthood on top of all that would be asking too much. In any case, in most capitalist countries there are regulators and consumer groups whose purpose is to restrain the wilder impulses of entrepreneurs.

Enterprise is the most important factor of production since in its absence it would be impossible to mobilise the other factors: labour, natural resources, capital and technology. People who study entrepreneurship focus on the notion of alertness – the ability to spot business opportunities in the most unlikely places. I experienced a good example of this in the United States in the early 1980s. In an idle moment in McDonald's, I made an aeroplane out of the polystyrene packaging. My children had great fun with it. A stranger rushed over and said I should submit the idea to McDonald's. He gave me his card and I reciprocated. I put the idea out of my head – it was all a little embarrassing – but he called a week later and insisted that I submit the idea. There was great competition between the different fast food outlets at the time and they were all looking for inexpensive gimmicks. To cut a long story short, we very nearly got lucky. Three questions stayed with me. One, does that kind of alertness to opportunity exist in Ireland? Two, if it did, would the 'inventor' take the risk of embarrassment by submitting the idea? Three, would the man who spotted the opportunity not pursue it on his own without involving the 'inventor'?

The evidence, such as it is, suggests that the Irish gene pool does not produce entrepreneurs in great numbers and that our culture does not nurture them. As noted in the last chapter, we tend to favour soft options. The Celtic Tiger was driven in the main by American enterprise which underlay the US multinationals that set up here. By contrast, we are blessed with extraordinarily talented people in the arts, especially literature and music, and in sport and broadcasting. Craft-work and various types of cottage industry appeal to us, and in this regard we have much in common with French Canadians. Like the Scots, we also produce world-class engineers and doctors, and have a fairly impressive tradition in the natural sciences. Irish soldiers and officers have a high reputation in international peace-keeping and in earlier years proved themselves on different battlefields around the world.

There are, of course, several excellent 'home-grown' entrepreneurs of note, but hardly enough to keep the economy going without the multinationals. It used to be said that the only way to make money in Ireland was by means of matrimony, alimony and parsimony. This is clearly an exaggeration, but it may indicate a belief that in some ways the cards were stacked against setting up a viable business, especially in a rural area. In a way, farmers are our original entrepreneurs and over the years they have shown remarkable flexibility in moving out of certain types of production into other forms when profitability warranted it. However, they did not as a rule significantly increase the total output from year to year, and yields per acre tended to remain low by European standards. It was found that bachelor farmers had the lowest overall productivity, married farmers came somewhere in the middle, while farmers who were renting land had the highest productivity – though still not all that impressive by European standards. The small scale of operations had something to do with this, but, in general, Irish farmers did not display very dynamic entrepreneurship.

There is a school of thought which argues that contented people have no need of progress. It seems a little unlikely that Irish people would fall into this camp. There is another theory, put forward by Edward de Bono,[1] which may be of more relevance. He argues that language can be a barrier to progress because old perceptions and concepts are frozen into language like fossils. Love of language, therefore, can confine us to viewing life in an old-fashioned way. Is Ireland's deservedly high reputation for literature antithetical to progress and entrepreneurial activity? Several literary figures, including John Montague, have observed that if you throw a stone over a hedge in Ireland, you'll hit a poet.

Many entrepreneurs say that they tend to operate on an intuitive, rather than a cognitive, basis. This is interesting because it isn't meant to happen like that! Entrepreneurs are supposed to weigh up the risks and rewards in a logical and rational way, rather than behave impulsively. The potential entrepreneur can somehow imagine the product or service and their role in developing it. An awful word, 'imagineering', is sometimes used to describe this process.

If we are timid to start with, however, a strong imagination may actually prevent us from starting our own businesses. We can imagine failure just as vividly as success. Our collective fear of nuclear energy, for example, is such that no one even wants to debate the issue. It is a mortal sin *in pectore*. There is something deeply 'cultural' going on here.

The finance minister of Grenada told me a story (just before the US invasion in 1983, which he predicted almost to the day). An American businessman visits the island and sees a local man sitting under a palm tree drinking coconut milk. He asks him how he can just sit there for hours on end doing nothing. The local man asks what he should be doing and the American tells him that he should be out working and making profit. The local man asks what he should do then. The American says he should reinvest the money and make more profit. 'And then what?' asks the Grenadian. 'More profit, more reinvestment,' the American says. 'And then what?' The American finally responds, 'Then you can go to a Caribbean island, sit under a palm tree and drink coconut milk!' The point of the story is that a country should follow its own culture. If the people enjoy leisure-time activities, are content, and are not particularly interested in making money, then why should anyone force them into becoming entrepreneurs?

Highly spiritual people – Tibetans, for example – are unlikely to place much emphasis on economic growth or on the affluence it brings. Indeed, it is amazing the number of American entrepreneurs who, in later life, turn to therapy, meditation and alternative religions, as if they regret how they have wasted their lives on making money. As the old saying goes, 'Not many people on their death-beds regret having spent too little time in the office.' It is also worth noting how many seriously rich people give their money away directly or by setting up foundations. As was noted earlier, philanthropy is not rational from a conventional economic perspective. Psychiatrists have suggested that the part of the brain which is stimulated as a result of doing good deeds is the same part that is affected by sexual activity. Maybe philanthropy should be the norm rather than the exception.

In Ireland of the twenty-first century the sturdy youths and comely maidens are no longer at the crossroads and, for good or ill, we have committed ourselves – or the government has committed us – to the philosophy of economic growth, and that clearly involves entrepreneurship. The record does not, however, assure us that we have a great deal of entrepreneurial talent.

In the thirty-five years since the first oil crisis, we have made little or no advance in developing energy substitutes, even though we are blessed with ample resources to produce energy from land, wind, waves and tides. A glance at the stock market listings shows that there are relatively few important companies under Irish control, and many of these are banks – institutions not renowned for entrepreneurship. Indeed, in 2008/09 our financial entrepreneurs have been shown up as complete failures. The same could be said of US bankers. Yes, but at least they invented new financial products. Our bankers did not invent anything; they made their huge mistakes in relation to good old-fashioned property. They engaged in a race to the bottom and displayed no entrepreneurial ability whatsoever. Yet the people who ran their banks into the ground were counted among our top entrepreneurs, as were many builders and property developers.

Israel has some seventy companies listed on the NASDAQ; by contrast, Ireland has only five. In general, it appears that we are still rather more interested in possessing than in performing – to use Joe Lee's famous phrase.[2] The availability of so many easy options, including EU money and foreign firms, may have retarded the development of an entrepreneurial culture in Ireland.

Family-run firms are still the norm and these tend not to grow beyond the point where the family might lose control. The owners are reluctant to hire professional managers, or go public, and they rarely want the hassle of exporting. These firms reach a certain size and then remain in that 'comfort zone'. It is amazing how many Irish-owned retail chains were sold off to foreign buyers. It is also intriguing how many British stores have opened in Ireland in the last ten years or so – Boots, Debenhams, Marks and Spencer, Argos, Tesco, Dixons. It is almost as if these British companies discovered an entrepreneurial vacuum in Ireland.

Brendan Behan once remarked that every meeting in Ireland begins with the split. It is certainly surprising how many different points of view can be raised around a meeting table in this country, and how difficult it can be to reach a decision through compromise. In multinational institutions like the IMF and World Bank, where there are some 180 different countries involved, and two or three times that number of cultures, it can often be easier to reach decisions. The reasons for the Irish situation are difficult to divine, but there may well be personal likes and dislikes involved, hidden agendas, or 'underground water' as the Irish phrase puts it. It sometimes seems as if no one plans, but everyone plots.

Perhaps we have difficulty separating business from personality. We may be easily distracted from the bottom line because we have a wide range of 'outside' interests. Maybe some people at meetings believe that certain decisions will reflect badly on them and they may lose face in front of their colleagues. Often if an argument goes against us, we regard it as an *ad hominem* attack and react accordingly. Losing face is more of a stigma in Asian countries, but it is not absent in Ireland. In a way, it is consistent with the zero-sum mind-set first advanced by Joe Lee.[3] This attitude harks back to the time when there was little or no development in Ireland, so whenever a decision had to be made, it meant that some people would get more of the pie and others less. There was no possibility that the pie itself would grow; consequently, there had to be losers. Hence the withering comment about Ireland by Yeats: 'Great hatred, little room.' All this baggage makes it difficult for entrepreneurs to function.

During the Celtic Tiger period, the pie was growing very quickly and this may have facilitated decision-making, but whether or not it has been embedded in the national psyche remains to be seen. Certainly, in recession we seem to be finding it very hard to agree on anything. Even the much-vaunted social partnership process broke down almost as soon as the going got tough. Each partner rushed to defend its own constituency without any regard for the common good. Opposition parties refused to ally themselves with the government because the latter would not admit that it did anything to cause the recession! As usual, tribal affiliations, and old-fashioned turf protection, prevented the emergence of a united front.

Whenever a multinational company leaves our shores, there is an understandable chorus of regret, followed by a demand that the Industrial Development Authority (IDA) and the government should set up a task force to bring in another company from abroad and so replace the jobs that were lost. It is common for a spokesperson from the local chamber of commerce or enterprise board to make this plea on behalf of their community. (What do these institutions actually do, apart from complain about job losses?) There is never the slightest suggestion that local entrepreneurship might come to the rescue, perhaps because it is recognised that this is inadequate or non-existent. The idea of self-help seems to be absent in many parts of the country. The emphasis is always on bringing another multinational firm into town, preferably straight into the recently vacated premises to avoid workers having to relocate. Lack of mobility may, in turn, have something to do with the well-documented 'sense of place'.

It has struck many people as odd that on St. Patrick's Day most of our senior politicians leave the country for the four corners of the world, especially the United States. It is a good marketing opportunity and sometimes when ministers return they announce jobs that will soon be created by an American or German company in Ireland. Several years ago I thought it would be a good idea if ministers spent more time abroad since they had this uncanny ability to persuade foreign companies to create jobs here. I did not realise in those innocent days that the IDA had already done the deals, but were not announcing them until the ministers were in a position to take the credit when they returned from their Patrick's Day visits! The point is that the long-established habit of trawling the world for jobs – and not just on our national day – is hardly a vote of confidence in domestic entrepreneurship. Depending on foreign business know-how for fifty years may not have empowered potential Irish entrepreneurs: on the contrary, they may have felt intimidated.

For years Irish entrepreneurs used to complain bitterly that they were unfairly treated in comparison with foreign multinationals. This view was correct and one wonders if domestic enterprise was somehow 'crowded out' back then. But the complaints died down when the low corporate tax rate was reduced in 1990 for all manufacturing companies, domestic as well as foreign. Some years later the tax rate for all companies, whether manufacturing or not, was harmonised at 12.5 per cent.

It is not being suggested that the entrepreneurial instinct is totally absent in Ireland. Indeed, there are many instances of courage and determination being displayed, often in poor economic circumstances. There was a very encouraging story some years ago. A man who lost his job as a white-collar worker was queuing up for the first time in a dole queue and he just could not accept it. He left the queue, sold his car, bought a van and set himself up as a gardener and landscaper. He now employs a staff of twelve. In Ireland, we often do respond well to adversity; it is success we sometimes have difficulty with. We do not hear these encouraging self-help stories very often.

A famous Hollywood actor once told a story about his difficulty with success. He could not believe that he had become a superstar and did not feel he deserved it. On one occasion he hyperventilated in a crowded restaurant and passed out. Other film stars who were present showered him with tranquillizers. Many had experienced similar symptoms. Fear of success can sometimes be as inhibiting as fear of failure.

For many years the jewel in Ireland's crown was Waterford Glass which, owing to poor management and a complacent dependency on a strong dollar, sought a loan guarantee from the government in 2009, which was rightly turned down. It seems extraordinary that such a request was made and it serves as a reminder of the 'infant-industry' days when entrepreneurship was so poor that government subsidies to private sector firms were quite common. It is certainly true that for many years the heads of companies devoted considerable amounts of time lobbying the authorities for grants. The Waterford Glass example suggests that the hand-out mentality is, surprisingly, still alive and well here. It also exemplifies how a wonderful company with a world-renowned product can be run into the ground.

Just before Christmas 2008, many shop-owners in Dublin and elsewhere complained bitterly that the different rates of VAT in Ireland and Britain were leading Irish consumers north of the border to do their Christmas shopping. Pressure was put on the government to lower the rate of VAT to 18 per cent in the Republic. It never seemed to occur to any store-owners that there was ample scope for them to lower their own margins, which for years had remained relatively high.

At some level this character flaw of looking outside ourselves for help was recognised by the architects of our economic take-off back in the late 1950s, who formulated the strategy of attracting in foreign direct investment and entrepreneurship. Since Ireland did not experience an industrial revolution, there was little else that could be done. The hope was that Irish people would learn entrepreneurial skills from the multinational companies, which were quite happy to mentor Irish firms. No doubt this happened to some extent, but it is clear that we are not yet self-sufficient where enterprise is concerned.

It is not surprising that a country so wounded by years of oppression would find it difficult to produce people of confident, risk-taking ability. After independence, the church and state acted as forces of conservatism, as Tom Garvin has shown.[4] The educational system was essentially run by the church and for many years little emphasis was given to technical or higher-level skills. In fact, the whole notion of material success was problematic for many people of a spiritual bent. Post-Famine feelings of guilt were probably also present. Redemption was more important than economic growth and increasing affluence. As one priest put it to his congregation who were drifting in late to evening benediction, 'You will have to choose between *Glenroe* and Jesus Christ'.

Parents encouraged their children to get secure jobs in the civil service. These were essentially jobs for life, and the 'lucky' job-holders would not have to deal with any risks for the rest of their careers. The emphasis on education led to a professional class that looked down its nose at people in business – often dismissed as 'chancers' and 'go-getters'. The great benefit of education was that it not only equipped sons and daughters for a good steady job, it also guaranteed them a decent social position. The latter was important to a people trying to achieve self-identity. Many of the 'chancers' emigrated to America and that of course depleted the enterprise gene pool at home. In the US, successful entrepreneurs are admired and emulated, while in Ireland there is still a tendency to envy them – although the old-style begrudgery seems to be less prevalent nowadays.[5]

For many years people with technical skills were not regarded as properly educated. The emphasis was very much on academic education and there was even a Newmanesque belief that a good education should not be utilitarian. In fact, academics in European countries were reluctant to become involved in applied science. America, by contrast, never had such cultural hang-ups and became the world leader in technology. Irish attitudes are now much more balanced, but it is still going to be difficult to compete with young Asian people, for example, who seem to have a natural aptitude for applied science. Asian people also tend to be extremely driven and hard-working; I have seen them in the science faculties of top American universities, power-napping in sleeping bags under their desks.

Entrepreneurs do not have to be scientists, of course, but they should be able to motivate scientists if we are to develop an information economy. A question arises in this regard. Why is it that the rewards to science teachers and researchers in Ireland aren't more attractive? The rewards available to bankers, lawyers and medical doctors are much greater than those available to scientists. A post-doctoral researcher in one of our top universities typically earns less than a policeman, brick-layer or prison warden. To some extent these market signals reflect the values of the society. Is it possible that, despite the protestations of the political spin doctors, we are not really all that interested in the information economy and that our emerging entrepreneurs are still looking at more old-fashioned businesses?

In a small, homogeneous society, there is nowhere to hide. If someone did take the risk of setting up a business, their failure would be apparent to everyone in the community. Irish people can be extremely kind to neighbours in trouble; indeed, the notion of sympathy is deeply rooted in the Gaelic tradition. Nevertheless, the prevailing attitude to someone who tries to rise above the norm can be very different. Even today in a small Irish town, setting up a business is like baring your soul or coming out of the closet. There can be even more embarrassment if the entrepreneurial idea is an unusual one. This runs counter to the good advice Einstein gave: 'If the idea is not at first absurd, then there is no hope for it.' In small communities in Ireland, it would require extraordinary bravery and self-confidence to be associated with absurd ideas.

In the 1950s, Irish farmers – the entrepreneurs of the time – would sometimes produce less if the price went up! The thinking behind it was that if prices for your output rise, then you can get away with producing less and still have the same standard of living. For many farmers of the time, leisure was preferable to work. Maybe religion or some form of asceticism lay behind the negative attitude towards a higher standard of living. It is possible that some version of this attitude survives among Irish entrepreneurs of today.

It is no surprise that the supremely confident Winston Chur-
chill once said, 'Success is the ability to go from one failure to
another with no loss of enthusiasm'. Irish people do not find it
so easy to shrug off failure or to take risks that may lead to failure. As we have been reminded by the fate of Seán Fitzpatrick,
bankruptcy is more punitive in Ireland than it is in the US, for
example.

We are not that comfortable in providing services to one another. Service tends to be equated with servility. It probably re-
minds us of when our great-grandmothers, or those of our
friends, were in domestic service in the big house. Selling
doesn't appeal to Irish people either; there is something de-
meaning about it, and of course a salesperson is always exposed
to rejection. A salesman once told me that to do the job properly, he had to learn how to take kicks in the teeth and continue
to smile. We don't even like using the word 'selling'; hence the
euphemisms 'marketing', 'product placement' and so on. We
may have the gift of the gab for selling, but not the confidence
or aggressiveness.

The infamous IDA hoarding that used to grace the arrivals hall
at Dublin airport annoyed many people because all the fresh-
faced Trinity students who appeared in it had already emigrated
to find work. The caption read: 'We are the young Europeans.
Employ us before we employ you.' But what was of even greater
import was the implication that these skilled youngsters would
prefer to be employees than entrepreneurs. The notion that they
might run their own companies was signalled only as a last resort,
that is, if they were not offered a job by a multinational company.
The reality was that they did neither; they emigrated.

Then, just as social and cultural norms were becoming
somewhat more welcoming to the emergence of an entrepreneurial class, at least in the cities, it transpired that the prevail-

ing model of enterprise was one of cunning and stroke-play. The emphasis was on making money for little or no effort, usually on the basis of cronyism and inside information. Risk-taking was for the race track, not for business. Profit was not the return on risk, but rather the pay-off for being well-connected or for owning some land that might be rezoned. The entrepreneurs who emerged in this period (the Haughey era) were not good role models for the next generation. Their legacy contributed to the property bubble and the economic collapse of 2008. This point was emphasised by Niall Fitzgerald in *The Irish Times* on 6 March 2010. He described the Irish business scene as 'claustrophobic' and one which 'militated against high ethical standards'.

There were many tax shelters provided for the rich, often related to property. A blind eye was turned to bogus non-resident accounts and straightforward offshore accounts. The rate of capital gains tax was halved at a stroke. Tax cheats were let off the hook by a number of amnesties. Regulations in the building trade were lax. Builders were allowed twelve years to complete the infrastructure of a housing estate. The wealthy were very well cosseted. The ostensible reason for this was the risk of 'capital flight', that is, the belief that if the wealthy were asked to pay more tax or subjected to too many regulations, they would move their capital out of the country. No doubt, this was a rationalisation for thinly disguised cronyism. This kind of environment was never going to lead to the emergence of genuine, hard-working entrepreneurs. Tax exiles, for example, do not create many jobs in Ireland.

There was also an element of *machismo* in that early form of entrepreneurship. Many of those who succeeded in business acquired horses, yachts and even football teams. I was aware of a regular game of golf where each member of the four-ball had to bet €10,000 on the round – with occasional side bets of a grand or so on six- or seven-foot putts. If this is how entrepreneurs have to let off steam, then so be it – as long as they continue to run successful businesses, employ people in productive work, and do not come running to government for hand-outs whenever they encounter problems. Many of those golden circle types became tax exiles as soon as they made big money. They were never entrepreneurs in the true meaning of the word. To paraphrase Fintan O'Toole, this rich group had the *noblesse* but not the *oblige*.

The *Freeman's Journal* once observed about the Irish character, 'Many are adept among the nimble-fingered tribe of sharpers, coiners, purse-snatchers and strolling prostitutes who stand thicker than onions in a bed.' In the eighteenth century the landed gentry looked down their noses at anyone in trade; nevertheless there is a tiny grain of truth in that unflattering characterisation. The lure of 'stroke-play' is still strong and seems to appeal to something in the Irish character. Unfortunately, there is very little communal value added by this type of behaviour.

One only has to listen to the Joe Duffy programme on RTE radio to discover that the country is still full of opportunists ready to 'gouge' the consumer at every hand's turn. Immigrant workers have been treated badly and underpaid by Irish employers who have sought to keep their profit margins as high as possible. Irish consumers have suffered at the hands of wholesalers and retailers, road hauliers, debt collectors, rogue builders and traders, property management companies, restaurateurs who pocket service charges, fashion model 'schools' which recruit innocent victims from the streets, lifestyle and semi-religious gurus who promise clients all sorts of self-improvements.

Partly because of this, almost every type of economic activity in this country is now regulated in one way or another. If one adds up the number of regulators, ombudsman's offices and other compliance bodies, the total is close to thirty. Regulation is also of the 'loose rein' or 'principles-based' variety; in other words, it is not nearly rigorous enough to make any difference to the prevailing venal mode of doing business in this country. The banking fiasco illustrates the point more than adequately.

Even in recession, many of our existing entrepreneurs are not averse to exploiting their customers whenever they can. Leaving business ethics aside, this is hardly a good strategy for the long term. If entrepreneurs hope to make a quick killing rather than foster the goodwill of their customers, it is unlikely they will stay in business for very long. Is this a throw-back to the days of the stroke – or further back to the days when it was necessary to pull the wool over the eyes of the landlord and his agents?

Are those entrepreneurs who sail close to the wind ethically the same ones who give large sums to charity? My suspicion is that there is a large overlap between the two groups. Many wealthy business people in Ireland have no compunction about cutting corners, avoiding or even evading taxes, but at the same time they make generous donations to charity. Economists might regard this as contradictory and impossible behaviour, but it exists. There is good and bad in everyone. Irish people dislike institutions like the Office of the Revenue Commissioners but can be quite generous when it comes to individuals who are down on their luck.

Allied to the reluctance to take genuine risks is the fear of accepting responsibility for decisions. This attitude prevents real change from occurring. Corporate executives are rarely sanctioned by their shareholders and most prefer a quiet life to a proactive, risky one. Corporate budgeting is often an exercise in minimising costs, rather than financing new ventures. Committees are frequently set up to spread the risks associated with decision-making; no individual has to carry the can if a decision is made collectively. Banks are reluctant to get involved in venture capital, especially for knowledge-based activities, but have had, until recently, little hesitation in lending for property or public houses.

The result is that during the decade from 1998 to 2008 the output of the indigenous manufacturing sector has been no more than 2 per cent per annum, or less than one-sixth of the performance of the foreign-owned sector. Also, as noted earlier, over 70 per cent of Ireland's exports come from foreign-owned firms located here. It was never a Celtic Tiger; it was an American one. A cultural theorist once observed rather bluntly that 'the Irish never saw the point of breaking their backs'.[6]

Politicians have argued that entrepreneurship is vibrant in Ireland, but this view is based on attitudinal data about people's *desires* to become entrepreneurs. It is almost entirely aspirational. In May 2006 I published a piece in *The Irish Times* raising the question of whether there was something in the national psyche that limited the stock of dynamic Irish entrepreneurs. The article provoked a strong response from the then Minister for Enterprise, Trade and Employment, Micheál Martin, who wrote a piece in response entitled 'The Flourishing Irish Entrepreneur'. He took me to task, saying that my (less sanguine) view 'had no place in twenty-first century Ireland', and that I was 'fundamentally mistaken'. This was before the crash – a time when realism was regarded as unpatriotic.

Naturally, there are improvements occurring every day and young people, especially those skilled in information technology, are capable of being good entrepreneurs. It does seem as if information technology plays to our strengths. But of course there is much more to the knowledge economy than sitting in front of a screen pushing a mouse around.

Despite those years of spectacular economic success, it is not clear that confidence in ourselves is as high as it should be. In the sporting world Irish teams prefer being underdogs. It is 'safer' not to have high expectations. There is evidence that Irish people can actually thrive in adversity, which somehow gets the adrenalin flowing. There is less distance to fall and no great loss of face. Sports fans, too, seem to share this attitude. One of Ireland's football chants still is, 'You can never beat the Irish'. This does not aspire to victory, but adopts the 'safer' defensive position of not losing.

Many Irish entrepreneurs hope to have a product that is so good it can sell itself. This reflects our difficulties with selling, but it might be that our rural background also reinforces this 'physiocratic' notion, that is, a preference to produce physical objects. In a world where intangible services are dominating the major economies, this is not a helpful attitude. However, it is usually more difficult to 'sell' intangible services. A friend once joined a firm of consultants; his first task was to cold-call a number of potential clients and convince them that they needed his firm's services. He sat looking at the phone for three days before he worked up the courage to make the first call.

I recall a version of this defensive posture at school. No one ever admitted that they studied hard; in fact, everyone cultivated the image of being a slacker. If you were seen to have worked hard and then didn't do so well in the exams, you had a good distance to fall. You might then be regarded as 'thick'. If, on the other hand, you were perceived as not being a good student but you did well in exams, then you would be seen as brainy. One astute character carried this pretence to extremes. He never brought home a book from school in case it would be inferred that he was doing extra study at home. He was regarded as very bright, until we found out that he had a duplicate set of books at home! This defensive attitude persisted into third level. The situation was completely different in British and American universities where students often *boasted* about how hard they were working. This came to me as a culture shock. No doubt such bizarre poses are less frequent in Ireland nowadays, but I would be surprised if they did not persist in certain parts of the country.

Since entrepreneurship is by far the most influential driver of real living standards, and because it is the glue that binds together all the factors of production, it is vital to understand how it operates if we are to make any attempt to assess our economic prospects over the next decade. Some countries – such as the United States, for instance – are naturally entrepreneurial and, assuming that animal spirits can be regulated, it is hard to see these countries coming to economic harm. For other cultures, entrepreneurship does not come so naturally and it has to be worked at. Confidence seems to be one of the essential ingredients and, for historical and other reasons, this may still be a difficult area for Irish people.

It is interesting to note that those activities where we excel – sport, music, literature, communications – give rise to surges of adrenalin which obliterate the effects of cultural baggage and allow us to give free rein to our natural ability. Confidence was probably built up to some extent during the Celtic Tiger period and it would be extremely damaging if it were lost in the current recession. The manner in which culture influences entrepreneurship will be a major determinant of our economic future.

5

THE UNDERPERFORMING PUBLIC SECTOR

'The public service serves you right.' – Adlai Stevenson, speech in Los Angeles, 1952

We have seen how economies are divided into three: incomes, spending and production. The three sides depend on each other. We cannot spend unless we earn an income and we cannot earn an income unless we produce (or work) and we cannot produce unless there is spending or demand. When something happens to interfere with this circular flow, whether caused domestically or externally, we may encounter recession.

Economies are usually subdivided into the private sector and the public sector. This is a useful distinction because these sectors behave differently. In trying to interpret overall economic behaviour, it is important to separate them.[1]

The public sector also includes people who earn income, spend and produce. They differ from their private sector counterparts in that they work for the state, produce goods and services for the community, such as currency notes, postage stamps, national security, policing, teaching and health services. The government usually has to raise taxes to pay these workers.

Generally speaking, the public sector does not work to make a profit, though there are exceptions.[2] But we expect our public servants to be entrepreneurial and efficient. Without the incentive provided by the profit motive, this may be asking a lot. It should also be remembered that the state is expected to provide social services as well as directly productive ones. For example, public transport can be productive (and profitable) in urban centres but becomes more of a social service in sparsely populated rural areas. In other words, the state decides to provide certain goods and services which private-sector entrepreneurs would not regard as profitable enough; the latter would cherry-pick the profitable parts and ignore the rest.

Quite some time ago, even before Reagan and Thatcher came to power, there were moves afoot in certain capitalist countries to minimise the role of the state precisely because of this lack of profit-driven efficiency. One way of doing that was to privatise state activities. In Ireland we followed suit – Telecom Éireann and Aer Lingus – and we are also flirting with public-private partnerships (PPPs), especially in health and affordable housing. There are several cases where the private-sector partner has pulled out because of recession. There is probably a limit to how far privatisation can go. It is hard to imagine armies and police forces being privatised, but one never knows how tight the grip of an ideology can become.

Years ago, little privatisation would have been possible because the private sector would not have been able to raise the capital. So-called 'lumpy' investment in electricity generation, railroads, canals and motorways, for example, had to be handled by the state. Now all these activities are up for grabs. Big multinational companies have the resources, and smaller companies can borrow from global capital markets. I have come across a situation where a multinational oil company occasionally gives its host country – a small country in the Caribbean – a cheque to balance its budget, in return for preferential tax treatment. This is a rather extreme example of the privatisation of government. Private companies will not provide loss-making social services, but they will tend to be more efficient. Hence, with privatisation, the taxpayer may gain but the consumer of the services could lose out. Governments should make prudent decisions about privatisation and should not be influenced by the prevailing ideology.

The idea that government should charge for the services it provides is a good one. The public does have to pay for several public services such as transport and visits to A&E wards. Many services are provided free, such as public parks, museums and art galleries. There is resistance to paying for services that once were provided free of charge. The idea of paying water and refuse charges seems to annoy many people. But what if we had to pay every time we called out a policeman or the fire brigade? The very idea is upsetting to most people, yet it has merit because it would prevent the frivolous use of costly services.

As was noted in earlier chapters, countries like Sweden and France tend to focus on the quality of service and on equity, while countries like the US and UK have gone for market-driven efficiency. Ireland is somewhere in the middle, though international bodies like the OECD, IMF and ECB tend to include us in the Anglo-American model of unfettered capitalism.

Table 2 sets out the important numbers pertaining to the public sector in Ireland.

Table 2: Numbers Employed in the Public Sector (000s End December, 2001-2008)

	2001	2008	% Change
Civil Service	36.1	39.0	+8.0
Health	93.0	111.0	+19.3
Education	73.3	92.8	+26.6
Defence	11.8	11.3	−4.2
Garda Síochána	12.5	15.4	+23.2
Local Authorities	32.0	34.8	+8.7
Semi-State Bodies (nc)	11.1	12.2	+9.9
Subtotal	269.8	316.3	+17.2
Semi-State Bodies (c)	47.7	41.3	−13.4
Total	317.5	357.6	+12.6

Notes: nc = non-commercial, c = commercial

At the end of 2008, Ireland employed 358,000 people in the public sector. At about 18 per cent of the total labour force, this proportion is not unduly high by international standards, though it must be remembered that most other countries are not neutral and have relatively large standing armies. Since salaries, on average, are higher in Ireland, the public sector pay bill would come to over 20 per cent of the total national pay bill.

If we add to this the value of other goods and services provided by government, we find that the total comes to over 40 per cent of GNP, about the same as the OECD average. In 2009, however, with falling GNP, our ratio has shot up to 50 per cent. The notion that government spending is a relatively low proportion of GNP in Ireland is a myth. (Low taxes are also a myth; it is true that income taxes until recently have been relatively low, but this has been more than compensated for by high indirect taxes, such as VAT, excise duties and Vehicle Registration Tax.)

The period covered in Table 2 goes from the end of the Celtic Tiger to the beginning of the recession. But even in this fairly 'normal' period, public sector numbers grew rapidly, especially in health, education and policing.

Does the public sector provide good value for money? Unfortunately, this question cannot be easily answered, partly because there is no measure of profitability. We cannot say whether or not any of the fifteen departments of state (which make up the bulk of the 'civil service') are profitable. The same is true for most of the 850 public bodies which they supervise. We hope that all these bodies give good advice to the government, and that this leads to sound policies and projects, but there is no easy way of determining this or of measuring the contribution they make to the economy.

In 2008 a report of the OECD[3] unfortunately did not benchmark the performance of the Irish public sector or audit any agencies, but simply looked at the lack of integration between different parts of the service. This report was also supervised during its preparation by a committee of senior civil servants. The Institute of Public Administration does not produce international benchmarks either, so it is difficult to tell precisely how efficient or inefficient the Irish public sector is. The Directory of State Services, which used to be produced by the Department of Finance, has not appeared in print for at least ten years!

What we have got to go on are the mistakes or delays which have been made in public projects over the years. The list is long, and it is hard to avoid the impression that during the splendid years of the Celtic Tiger, the private sector – certainly the foreign component – was delivering the goods, but the public sector let down the side. It is instructive to consider the long list of errors in a variety of sectors.

Health

Problems in the public health sector have cropped up with worrying regularity during the last decade and a half. These included excessively long waiting times in A&E wards where seriously ill patients were forced to wait on trolleys in corridors. There were scandals relating to contaminated blood, the retention of children's organs, infection caused by lack of hygiene in state hospitals, overcharging and mistreatment of elderly patients in nursing homes, poor diagnostic practices, misdiagnosis of breast and other cancers, misinterpretation of foetal images and inexplicable surgical practices, especially in relation to hysterectomies. In early 2010 it emerged that almost 60,000 X-rays in the flagship Tallaght hospital had not been reviewed by a consultant radiologist. It also came to light that some 3,000 letters from GPs concerning their patients had remained unopened in the same hospital.

A promise to provide vaccination against cervical cancer was withdrawn in 2009, though later introduced, following protests. No hospitals had special wards or bathrooms for infectious diseases such as cystic fibrosis. Transplantable organs were frequently sent for use abroad because beds could not be found for Irish patients who needed those organs. Life expectancy for people with chronic medical conditions tended to be low by international comparison.

Social workers and other members of the caring professions made mistakes that had tragic consequences. The provision of after-hours care is virtually non-existent. The Health Service Executive (HSE) admitted that in the six years from 2004 to 2010, 23 children in care died. After a long delay this figure was raised to 37 and, later on, to 131. In June 2010 the estimate reached 188. Some commentators argued that the figure could be substantially higher if a wider definition were used. A report on one of these tragic cases was revealed by a member of the Fine Gael party in March 2010; it is not clear that the HSE, left to its own devices, would ever have published any report. In fact, its files on these tragic cases leave a lot to be desired. The national Ombudsman, Ms Emily O'Reilly, has criticised the HSE in the stongest terms.

An appalling case came to light in 2010: six children of the same family had been abused by both parents over a fifteen-year period while the HSE stood idly by. This was followed by the revelation that over a third of foster parents in the southern part of the country had never been properly vetted by the HSE. The incidence of suicide increased to about 500 cases a year – an unprecedented level. In 2009, a secure facility for troubled children – built only ten years earlier – had to be closed down. There are frequent reports about the mistreatment of intellectually disabled people in state-run institutions. These dreadful and tragic facts speak for themselves.

It took years to decide on the location of a national children's hospital and even now, in 2010, there are still serious reservations about the chosen Mater site. It took six years to negotiate a new contract with hospital consultants and, because of budgetary difficulties in 2010, it may have to be altered. The merging of the different health boards clearly did not work and the increase in staff numbers by almost 20 per cent (to 111,000 in 2008) made little difference. It is notable in this regard that doctors and dentists combined came to only about 5 per cent of the total staffing, a very low proportion by international standards. On the other hand, the numbers of managerial, administrative and nursing staff are exceptionally high. The quality of care is affected by high absenteeism and part-time working. Patients' rights do not have a high priority.

It is also worth noting that the HSE staff of 111,000 does not include the staff of the Department of Health and Children, which numbered 526 in 2008. This Department is mainly responsible for health policy, but it is difficult to understand why this function should require over 500 staff. The relationship between the Department and the HSE leaves much to be desired.

Expenditure on health in Ireland as a percentage of GNP is about average by comparison with OECD countries, and the number of hospital beds per 1,000 of the population is not noticeably low. Clearly there are structural, procedural and industrial relations problems within the health sector which have not yet been resolved. Whether or not the approach to centres of excellence will work is still an open question, as is the government's aim of introducing public-private partnerships (co-location) into the health sector.

Policing and Justice

Although crime statistics are notoriously hard to interpret, it is clear that serious crime in Ireland has increased enormously in recent years. Drug-related murders have been rising steadily. In 2007 there were 84 murders or manslaughters, 25 per cent up on the previous year. Drink- and drug-related assaults of a vicious nature are far too frequent. Only 10 per cent of police are on duty at any given time – a low ratio by international standards. The high proportion of police checking on driving licences and doing paperwork is a clear misallocation of resources. The so-called 'blue flu' in 1998 was an episode that many people regarded as one of near anarchy, but one that resulted in no sanction by government. The fact that taxi-drivers were allowed to block the entire Dublin city centre for two days in October 2009 without any intervention by the gardaí speaks volumes. Later that year, the gardaí considered industrial action, despite a constitutional bar on such action.

There have been scandals, especially in County Donegal (investigated by the Morris Tribunal) and in Abbeylara, County Longford, and the establishment of an ombudsman commission was resisted for many years. Every decision by senior management, or even by the government – such as the recruitment of a police reserve, the establishment of an armed response unit – is questioned by the Garda Representative Association.

The courts are congested and allow bail too easily. A high proportion of murders are committed by criminals who have been granted bail. Many sentences are too short, and space constraints in prisons have given rise to a policy of early release.

The role of the Director of Public Prosecutions has been questioned, especially the fact that he does not have to explain his decisions. There have been a couple of scandals involving judges and several instances of politicians trying to influence judicial decisions. In general, the victims of crime are treated extremely badly in this country. Sentencing policy is uneven and unpredictable; in early 2010, a convicted paedophile who had been charged with 189 offences was given a custodial sentence of only four years.

As far as civil cases are concerned, the judicial process is slow and cumbersome – made even more dilatory by the number of barristers doing work for the various tribunals of inquiry. The Department of Justice has ducked responsibility by stating on numerous occasions that the courts service is an autonomous body. Because of the extraordinary costs involved, it is almost impossible for any individual to take a case to the High Court, and the legal system prevents class actions. In July 2010 the Taxing Master reduced legal fees in a civil case by 82 per cent, stating that the original demand for €2.1 million was 'revolting in the extreme'.

Corporate law needs to be substantially revised. At present it is used to provide protection for the directors of limited companies. For example, during the building boom, most big builders and developers set up a company for each project. No bonds were required and the sub-contractors had no liens on the buildings. When a particular company went bankrupt, the sub-contractors were left high and dry. They had no recourse to the builder or the developer, who were protected by limited liability and whose assets could not be used to pay the sub-contractors.

Even when serious criminals are jailed, they are able to access drugs and mobile phones. This is not because of a shortage of prison officers. On the contrary, there is one prison officer for every prisoner. Prison visitors routinely bring drugs into prisons and are rarely detected. A crackdown on mobile phones occurred in 2008 only because an inmate called a phone-in radio programme! So what exactly had been going on in prisons before that? Why had so much tolerance been shown to prisoners who were known to be using mobile phones to run their criminal enterprises, and even to order assassinations on the outside?

Some years ago the prison officers' staff association did a deal with para-military prisoners whereby the latter would be treated well by the prison officers on condition that the Provos would not target the prison officers or their families. A former representative of the staff association spoke openly about the arrangement on radio long after the event. It is not known if the state was aware of this arrangement at the time, but it could have established a dangerous precedent. There is anecdotal evidence to the effect that the forces of law and order are sometimes neutralised by threats made by organised crime bosses.

Driving offences, including drink-driving, are treated leniently by the courts. This partly explains why deaths and serious accidents on roads are high in Ireland. A government decision, reached in late 2009, to tighten up on drink-driving could not be implemented for 18 months because it was discovered that the existing alcohol-measuring equipment was not up to the task. It took 12 years to erect speed cameras here.

Despite various tribunals of inquiry, white-collar crime and corruption effectively go unpunished in Ireland. Partly because of the recent banking fiasco and light-touch regulation, this has earned Ireland the unfortunate soubriquet of 'the wild west'. The US crime of 'civil racketeering' does not appear on our statute books and it is almost impossible to prove that an act of fraud was committed. The white-collar establishment in Ireland is very strong and looks after its own.

Education

Education is a sector where resources have been increased dramatically but, again, it is very difficult to measure their effectiveness. The first budget of 2009 implied a slight increase in pupil–teacher ratios at primary level and this brought forth major complaints from teachers. The government responded that international evidence suggests that pupil–teacher ratios are not as important as the quality of the teachers. Unfortunately, this cannot be measured and the teaching profession is reluctant to submit to frequent inspections. Three of the main teachers' unions have rejected the proposal that schools be graded and the results published.

As noted earlier, there is evidence of grade inflation at secondary school level. Despite this, the failure rate in mathematics is increasing at an alarming rate. This means that many students are going on to third-level without the requisite skills. Given the urgent need for science-based education, it is surprising that teachers of mathematics and science are not paid more than their peers. Although this would be divisive within the teaching profession, it is almost certain to happen if the government is serious about its plan to transform Ireland into a 'smart' economy. The emphasis on rote learning is not consistent with the need to develop a capacity for innovation. In early 2010 the chief executives of some multinational companies raised questions about the quality of recent graduates and the possibility of grade inflation.

The physical infrastructure has not been maintained and many schools are sub-standard, depending on prefab huts to cope with an increase in student numbers which the authorities for some reason had not predicted. The increase in population in dormitory areas near Dublin – Counties Meath, Kildare, Wexford and Laois – has put further pressure on schools. This trend could, of course, be reversed if large-scale emigration continues during the recession.

The state training agency, FÁS, was subject to scrutiny in 2008. The Controller and Auditor General raised several questions, and subsequent inquiries revealed an organisation that was badly run, did not do the important job it was set up for and had very lax expenditure control systems, especially where the expenses of senior executives were concerned. This agency managed to spend €1 billion per annum, even when the country had practically no unemployment. More seriously still, several qualifications were improperly awarded to trainees. The fact that such lax practices went undetected for so long in one of the most important public bodies raises serious questions about standards in state agencies.

Infrastructural Projects

Poor, and sometimes corrupt, urban planning has led to urban sprawl in many cities, especially Dublin where the area covered by low-density housing is as large as that of many cities in the world with three or four times Dublin's population. During the building boom, many huge estates were built on the outskirts of Dublin with totally inadequate transport and school facilities. The costs of urban sprawl in commuting time, nervous energy and carbon emissions are enormous.

After severe rains in 2010, many new housing estates were flooded, and it emerged that the houses had been built on flood plains. How such planning errors were made has still not been investigated. After the property crash many housing estates around the country have become ghost estates, a number of which may have to be demolished.

It is generally accepted that the infrastructure – roads, rail, airports, shipping ports – are not up to standard for an economy at Ireland's stage of development. Errors and cost overruns have occurred in nearly every large project undertaken. The Luas tram project went way over time and budget and resulted in two sets of rail lines that were not connected. One line compounded traffic gridlock in several places, especially at an already congested roundabout.

Dublin's port tunnel went way over budget and had many teething problems; the question of safety has still not been resolved with the fire service. Roofs have blown off a new aquatic centre at Abbotstown. A project to build a new prison got off to a bad start when an excessive price was paid for the land. Problems with the M50 motorway around Dublin are legion, the fundamental mistake being one of inadequate scale at the planning stage. Related to this was the deal done with the tolling company which represented extremely bad value for the taxpayer. To date, road improvement simply results in a shifting of jam points and not their elimination. In many cases, the safety barriers along the medians are not up to EU safety standards. In addition, the cost per kilometre of carriageway is over twice the cost in OECD countries. Many of the new motorways lack service stations and rest areas.

Other projects, such as the Punchestown racecourse and the government's contribution to the completion of the new Croke Park, were not subjected to any analysis and the decisions behind them could be described as capricious. Building the M3 roadway so close to the ancient heritage site of Tara is an act of cultural and environmental vandalism which has attracted amazed disbelief from many other countries. Flood defences are inadequate in many parts of the country and way behind schedule. These deficiencies led to widespread flooding and extreme hardship in the west and south of the country in December 2009. Insurance claims alone will probably exceed €250 million and give rise to an increase in premia.

At the start of 2010 a cold spell of weather brought the country to a standstill. The local authorities and the National Roads Authority failed to grit the roads. Various excuses were given, ranging from budget cuts to a shortage of grit. Nothing had been learnt from a much colder period of weather in 1982. No one agency accepted responsibility.

There have been serious difficulties with water supply, especially in Galway, where people spent months on end using bottled water. There were subsequent contaminations in Waterford. The floods at the end of 2009 caused further problems throughout the country. One of the main contributing factors was slurry run-off which has poisoned lakes, rivers and aquifers, but there were also serious instances of lead contamination. We are now being told that, despite the high rainfall in Ireland, we are likely to run short of water in a few years. This is bizarre, given the weather in Ireland compared with countries like Israel, which has no difficulty piping water from Lake Galilee. Our problems are man-made: the infrastructure has not been properly maintained. A staggering 50 per cent of clean water leaks from old pipes into the ground, and most local authorities have no idea where these leaks occur. Some state-of-the-art sewage treatment plants are not working properly.

There is also a deficit in what might be termed intellectual infrastructure, and this is inconsistent with the explicit policy goal of becoming a leading information economy. Broadband technology is still limited, Ireland's R&D spend is one of the lowest in the developed world, and market signals regarding pay prospects encourage students to take non-science subjects.

General Administration

Many errors have occurred under this heading as well. The hoped for change to electronic voting ended in disaster, as did several other public sector computer installations (gardaí and health). In the transport sector, integrated ticketing has been promised for years but has not appeared. A vast number of quangos and public bodies have been set up in recent years, bringing the total – including local authorities, other regional agencies and task forces – to an incredible 850. Many of these bodies are not accountable and most have political appointees at their helm. It is far from clear how efficient the regulatory bodies are. The financial regulator was unable to prevent or mitigate the banking crisis in 2008. The taxi regulator put up taxi fares by 8 per cent in 2009, even though most taxi-drivers thought fares should be lower in a recession! The energy regulator prevented the Electricity Supply Board (ESB) from reducing electricity prices!

There has been no audit of the efficiency of departments of state or of the bodies they supervise. Some of these departments have been hollowed out by delegating work to other agencies, but the 'legacy' departments have made little effort to reduce staff numbers. One wonders what value for money we derive from many of our 60 embassies in foreign countries, or from various state-run monopolies which treat customers with contempt and are outside the remit of the National Consumer Agency. Why was no effort made over a period of about 15 years to limit the extraordinary legal fees incurred by the tribunals of inquiry?

Benchmarking of the public sector for the purpose of awarding pay increases was unscientific and resulted in excessive pay awards. Bonus schemes in the public sector tend not to be based on performance differentials. Senior public officials, as well as ministers, are among the highest paid in the world, even though the most important policy decisions are made in Brussels, Frankfurt, Silicon Valley and Washington DC. The system of unvouched expenses for politicians symbolises the laxity where taxpayers' money is concerned.

In late 2009, when ministers were examining their own departmental budgets in an attempt to make spending cuts that would not be too painful, it emerged that social welfare fraud could amount to some €2 billion a year. This extraordinarily high figure was estimated by RTÉ and it was not really challenged by the minister in question. It beggars belief that this level of fraud could have been allowed to continue over the years. It is hardly an exaggeration to say that if it had been

clamped down on, we would not now have to face such extreme
budgetary difficulties.

Generally speaking, the style of administration owes more to
public relations and spin than to tackling issues in a substantive
way. The civil service has become politicised over the years. This
means that there is little, if any, really independent advice being
offered to ministers, who, in any case, have several personal
advisers appointed by themselves.

Policy Errors

Errors under this heading are potentially the most costly of all,
but the media tend not to highlight them. Over the last ten
years the stance of fiscal policy was pro-cyclical when it should
have been the opposite.[4] In most of these years the Department
of Finance proved unable to forecast government revenue to any
acceptable degree of accuracy. Government spending grew
excessively, even though much of the tax base was ephemeral.

In the early 1980s, the Department of Finance presided over
an untenable situation of excessive borrowing and fiscal
deficits which was leading the country into bankruptcy. When
politicians eventually decided to call a halt, the department
had to hire consultants ('An Bord Snip') to cut public spending
which had been out of control on their watch. A standard joke
in the Department of Finance was that if the government's
credit-worthiness failed, it could always 'sell the *Asgard*'. It may
be merely symbolic, but the *Asgard* sank in the Bay of Biscay
on 11 September 2008.

In 2008, a second 'Bord Snip' was brought into the
Department of Finance to perform even more radical surgery on
public spending which had, yet again, spiralled out of control. So
no lessons were learnt from the previous experience, and
nothing has really changed, except that the department's

forecasts of revenue, expenditure and indeed the economy as a whole are worse than ever. It is sobering to realise that this is the 'premier department' of the public sector.[5]

Since T.K. Whitaker and Charles Murray left the Department of Finance in the early 1970s, there has been no serious attempt to formulate macroeconomic policy in a coherent way. During the Whitaker era, indicative planning was at its height – to the extent that a ministerial speech at the time contained the phrase 'not to plan is planning by default'. With the passing of the Whitaker era, not only did planning fall by the wayside but the prevailing economic ethos was abandoned in favour of general administration. Many top-flight economists left the department in subsequent years and were never replaced. No other treasury in the world ever attempted to perform its duties with so little economic expertise.

Our reliance on foreign direct investment was a soft option which worked well but created unrealistic expectations. The development of the International Financial Services Centre was widely hailed at its inception in the late 1980s but, given the number of brass plate operations there at present, light regulation, and the tax-harvesting that occurs, it could well become something of a liability. Other countries are beginning to complain about their exchequers losing corporate profit tax revenue. There has even been a suggestion that the International Financial Services Centre may have contaminated the regulation of domestic banks which also lobbied for light-touch regulation.

If foreign direct investment were to slow down, then our long-standing growth policy would become redundant, and there is nothing to replace it. Again, there is no plan B. This is because the public sector does not examine other strategies – or 'what if' scenarios – which in other countries are regarded as crucial for policy-making.

Financial regulation failed hopelessly to prevent or mitigate a meltdown of the Irish banking system in late 2008. Even when it became obvious that there was a bubble in the property market, the authorities failed to act. Then they flatly denied there was a problem in the banking sector – a problem that was home-grown since Irish banks did not have any US sub-prime assets on their books. Eventually an enormous deposit guarantee of some €450 billion had to be put in place, followed by substantial recapitalisations, one nationalisation and, finally, NAMA. It must be noted that all the members of the financial regulatory authority were political appointees, as were most of the directors of the Central Bank. The various interventions by government did little to impress international markets. It is not clear how NAMA will actually function on a day-to-day basis. It is likely that the taxpayer will have to pick up a substantial tab when all the distressed assets are disposed of. This, combined with the €24 billion which has been injected into Anglo Irish Bank, is creating huge tension between the social partners at a time of fiscal retrenchment. This tension will become even more severe if the banks continue to refuse credit to many small businesses. Ironically, the banks might decide to lend (their ECB funds) to government rather than to the private sector. Despite this, however, Ireland's ability to borrow abroad from private markets will remain circumscribed – and more expensive because of a substantial risk premium.

Free third-level education was a policy error because it mainly subsidised the middle classes, who could afford to pay fees. There was no attempt to target lower socio-economic groups, who, in effect, were subsidising the middle classes. The policy was introduced for crass political reasons. Basically, the government of the day lacked the courage to force farmers to present a true picture of their income for purposes of means-testing.

Since communication is one of our strengths, it is strange that we do not have a higher diplomatic profile internationally, or that we do not provide senior people to help mediate international disputes. One explanation may be that Irish diplomats tend to model themselves on the British and French formal style which does not come naturally to us, and which does not impress many nations of the world nowadays.

National pay agreements, to which the Irish government was a major signatory, resulted in a loss of competitiveness in the economy. The agreements never took into account the risks that lay dormant even during the good years – one of the major ones being that we no longer had the exchange-rate as a policy instrument. It was jam today in the hope of jam tomorrow. Responsibility for this probably rests with various taoisigh rather than with the ministers for finance. It is noteworthy that relations between the two respective departments leave much to be desired. It was C.J. Haughey who beefed up the Department of An Taoiseach in the early 1980s, and from then on there was an uneasy power relationship between that department and the Department of Finance.

The first 2009 budget was based on very shaky forecasts regarding economic and revenue growth. By imposing a levy on the low-paid, it was inconsistent with the agreements already reached with the social partners. Because of many insensitive provisions, the budget began to unravel within days of its announcement. Another budget had to be cobbled together for 2009. Perhaps a little more thought went into the 2010 budget, but despite some €4 billion in planned expenditure cuts, the deficit will remain high and the target deficit (3 per cent of GDP in 2013) is not likely to be achieved until 2014, or later.

There is as yet no sign of a medium-term economic strategy, and questions are being asked about whether or not the government and the Department of Finance have the ability to produce a joined-up plan.

It is reasonable to assume that the degree of enterprise within the public sector is less than in the private sector. People who enter the public service tend to be more interested in security than in risk-taking, more adept at administration than analytical or innovative work. In addition, the factors listed below were present to one degree or another.

Lack of Skills

The public sector does not try very hard to recruit or retain skilled staff. An OECD study[6] describes the Irish public service as a career-based rather than a position-based one. The US and UK fall into the latter category – which depends on in-house expertise – and these are the two capitalist models that Ireland is closest to. Yet for some reason Ireland has chosen a completely different type of public sector – one that cannot seem to cope with the needs of a growing market-driven economy. Why? First, it reflects what has been suggested earlier about Ireland's pragmatic, ad hoc style of governance. Second, the civil service fears skilled specialists. Whenever it has to recruit them – for example, architects in the Office of Public Works, or veterinarians in the Department of Agriculture – it sets a limit to their career paths. The top jobs are invariably reserved for general, non-specialist staff, many of whom would have joined the departments in question on leaving secondary school. The dictum is, 'Experts on tap but never on top'.

Economists had their moment in the sun when T.K. Whitaker ran the Department of Finance (1955–1969). Indeed, he frightened the system by saying that a fast career track should be available to econometricians! But as soon as he left the department in 1969, all that 'economic planning nonsense' was

ended, and the general administrators were back in pole
position. (I often wondered if those impressive public servants,
such as Ken Whitaker and Charlie Murray, ever became aware of
how quickly their important influence waned.) It should not
come as a surprise that fiscal policy since then was poorly
designed or that forecasts of government revenue were nearly
always wide of the mark.

Economics did make a partial comeback when a new
Department of Economic Planning and Development was set up
in 1977. This was anathema to the Department of Finance, which
lost a lot of its powers to the new department. And it put an end
to the development of capital appraisal – a system that is still
desperately needed. There was a lot of duplication between the
two departments – even at meetings abroad – sometimes to an
embarrassing degree. Finance breathed a sigh of relief when the
new department was abolished by C.J. Haughey in 1979, and the
status quo restored.

One of the few departments where specialists can and do rise
to the very top is the Central Statistics Office. But the top official
of that organisation is not remunerated at secretary-general level!
He or she is kept at a notch below. It has often been suggested
that the public sector should hire skilled people from the private
sector or from academia. This is unlikely to happen, for the
simple reason that senior civil servants do not look favourably on
anyone earning more than themselves. A partial solution to this
problem is hiring on contract. It does not bother senior civil
servants so much if highly paid specialists are on a contract since
they will not be around long enough to pose a career challenge.

Declining Focus on the Public Interest

There was a time when the concept of the public interest
seemed to matter to civil servants. When I joined the

Department of Finance in the late 1960s, all the administrative officers were sent to the Institute of Public Administration on a seven-week course. This was the enlightened Whitaker period. We had lecturers from every walk of life, even a moral philosopher and political scientist from UCD who drilled into us the moral obligation of working for the national interest. We were told that if we were not motivated by the common good, we should leave the civil service and get a job in the private sector where self-interest was the norm.

Those of us who had studied economics in UCD had been told that already by lecturers like Paddy Lynch and Garret FitzGerald. We were never going to earn huge salaries, but we had an opportunity of doing something for the country. When I was stuck in the personnel division of the Department of Finance, trying to decide whether a clerical officer should be compensated for laddering her tights on an in-tray, I often wondered how exactly my decision would help the national interest. Although one was expected to write long and elegant memos on such matters, I soon learned that this was make-work. The essential thing was to say 'no' as often and as strongly as possible. So when a claim from an ambassador landed on my desk, I went through it in great detail. An accident had occurred at the embassy abroad and the ambassador was seeking compensation for personal possessions that had been damaged. Armed with my recent understanding of departmental philosophy, I rejected about half of the claim – and in turn was overruled by my boss on the grounds that an ambassador was 'one of our own'! So, even then, the ideal of putting the country first might have been more apparent than real.

Years later, at a conference, the then secretary-general of the Department of Finance argued passionately that civil servants in Ireland did not conform with Niskanen's theory of the bureaucrat.[7] On the contrary, Irish civil servants were motivated solely by the public interest and, if they were to be criticised at all, it would be for 'excessive zeal'. Most of those attending the conference were public servants and the entire hall swayed with barely suppressed laughter. The vast majority of public officials in that room simply did not believe any longer that the national interest was a guiding star.

One result of this failure is the casual attitude towards taxpayers' money. When civil servants need to buy products or services from private companies, they tend not to shop around or to 'bargain'. Private suppliers are delighted whenever they land a public contract because they can add a substantial margin to the cost quoted. The chances are that it will not even be queried. This has serious implications for public-private partnerships (PPPs). The state should ensure that the private sector partner does not exploit the situation. Even if the private sector is more efficient than the public sector, it will not benefit the taxpayer if there is overcharging. Morale and skill problems clearly weaken the negotiating position of the public-sector side of the partnership.

Poor Morale

There are several reasons why morale in the public service has been undermined in recent years. Government intervention in the running of the civil service, and the use of political advisors and/or programme managers, constitute one reason. In recent years ministers have hardly been inspiring or demanding. This often has a 'dumbing down' effect. At the simplest level, if a civil servant is invited to a meeting in the minister's office and he knows the minister is going to chat about the weather or a recent hurling match, he is not going to do much preparatory work. Hence the phrase, 'Easy minister, easy life'.

The management of civil servants has tended to be 'old school'. For example, if mistakes are made, especially numerical ones, the miscreant is usually punished in one way or another. In departmental jargon, he is kicked up the backside. I was at a course on one occasion where the management guru was telling us that we needed to encourage people to admit their mistakes and if they learned from them they should be rewarded. It was all too much for a senior colleague who got up and walked out of the room. It was the worst heresy he had ever heard. As a young civil servant, he had been kicked up the backside; as a manager, he had no intention of changing the system.

Probably the most devious punishment was to put a note of censure on an individual's personnel file without telling them. If and when they were passed over for promotion, they would never know why. Probably the worst rebuke was to tell wrongdoers that their mistake had caused the minister to 'jump up and down'. Civil servants of a nervous disposition often think the minister is jumping up and down even when he or she is perfectly still.

The treatment of women was particularly bad in the old days. Women civil servants were discouraged from seeking promotion or entering competitions on the grounds that 'the men would look after them'. Many of these women, who are now nearing retirement, were never 'looked after' and they have no power under the equality legislation because it is not retrospective. It has always been a source of amazement that the women's movement has not examined this problem. The equality legislation is in fact ageist!

In 1999 the public accounts committee investigation into bogus non-resident accounts, under the chairmanship of the late Jim Mitchell TD, saved the taxpayer a considerable sum of money. However, by excluding ministers and other politicians from the process, and by targeting public officials only, it delivered a hammer blow to morale in the civil service. Several senior civil servants were humiliated by being interrogated in a very public manner. A partial solution was discovered. If women civil servants were sent in to bat at these Oireachtas committees, the politicians could not afford to harass them in the full glare of publicity. Many women were promoted in the civil service for this very reason.

When the plan to decentralise the civil service was announced by Charlie McCreevy in his budget speech of 2000, there was consternation among public officials. There had been no consultation of any sort and civil servants felt that they were being pushed around like pawns in a chess game. The decentralisation plan ignored the national spatial strategy, designed to help the regions in the twenty-year period up to 2020. That strategy had been worked on enthusiastically by many officials. The fact that it was so capriciously set aside for short-term political gain was an additional blow to morale.

Lack of Independent Advice

Under the strategic management initiative of 1998, a top level appointments commission was set up, but it was undermined by politicians almost from the word go. Instead of the commission recommending the best candidate for a senior position, it was forced to present three names to the political higher-ups. This was one of the methods by which the system was politicised. But would it really help a Fianna Fáil minister if his senior advisors had the same party affiliations? Would there not be a tendency to tell the minister what he wanted to hear?

A common sight nowadays is that of senior civil servants carrying a minister's luggage and duty-free purchases through airports, or getting them plates of food from buffet tables, or holding umbrellas over their heads. It seems as if deference has taken over from hard-nosed, independent advice.

Senior civil servants are reluctant to make strong, unambiguous recommendations. Without skilled analysts, of course, it is difficult to come to any decisions with confidence. The fear is that if the recommendation were implemented, it might come back to haunt its proponent. That could affect career prospects, whereas inertia does not. This asymmetry is what perpetuates the dead hand of bureaucracy. Bob Hope once remarked: 'I don't know why everyone hates Jimmy Carter; he's done nothing.' That comment makes even more sense on this side of the Atlantic. Doing nothing is the best strategy for success. Hence the well-known quip: 'A good civil servant finds a problem for every solution.' Change is scary and there is no percentage in it. Civil servants are going to get their bonuses and increments anyway, whether they propose new ideas or not.

The emphasis is on accuracy, factual and statistical accuracy. If a wrong fact or number gets into a ministerial speech and is picked up on by the opposition, all hell can break loose. This is the official's worst nightmare, so a huge amount of resources goes into checking and rechecking. Content, ideas, innovation, none of this really matters. Very senior people spend far too little time on strategic issues. The urgent – as well as the need for accuracy – always drives out the important. I knew of at least two senior officials who would not fact-check a photocopy. They insisted on having the original – in case the photocopying machine had made a mistake. Accuracy is essential but when it becomes an obsession, it kills initiative.

Poor Decision-making

It has already been suggested that Irish people are not very decisive. If someone makes a decision, they should take responsibility for the outcome. In the Irish public sector, no one wants to take responsibility. There is never any question of a minister resigning. Senior civil servants certainly do not fall on their swords. Since ministers don't, why should they?

The refusal to take responsibility is built into the system. For example, the terms of reference of all senior committees will mention such terms as, 'advice', 'recommendation' and 'coordination'. The words 'decide' or 'decision' never appear. 'I'm not paid to make a decision' is a phrase one often hears in the so-called corridors of power. Everyone subscribes to the Woodrow Wilson dictum: 'If you want to make enemies, change something.' We don't want to make enemies.

There is also the fear of 'creating a precedent' or, in more feverish parlance, 'opening the flood-gates'. This is an irrational fear. If a good decision is worth making, then the precedent so created will also be a good one. This fear of precedent is a rationalisation of the reluctance to take any decision that will change the status quo.

Several experts have criticised the historical role of the minister as *corporation sole* which theoretically vested all responsibility in the minister. That never really worked, and it was treated as a legal fiction. Ministers did not accept that degree of responsibility. In the late 1990s, an attempt was made to share the burden by giving responsibility for day-to-day matters to secretaries-general. In practice that hasn't worked either. As has been noted already, most important economic decisions are made outside Ireland and this clearly suits the public sector.

Inability or unwillingness to take responsibility has led to most circuitous forms of decision-making, even about relatively unimportant matters. Committees are set up as *cordons sanitaires*; consultants are hired, and quangos and other public bodies are established in the hope that they will take responsibility for decisions. Everyone passes the buck. If you write to a minister about some matter, the reply will invariably refer you to a quango which is described as 'autonomous'. I have several of these letters. In reality, the quango in question is anything but autonomous; it is under the aegis of the minister and of his government department. But by describing it as 'autonomous', it is hoped you will go away, or contact the quango, in which case they will tell you the subject 'does not fall under our remit'. It is nothing to be referred on to six or seven different quangos, each one 'providing all assistance, bar help'. You will never get an answer, of course, but the art of buck-passing employs thousands of officials.

I sometimes wonder if the system is designed to make the citizen go to the minister's political clinic, throw himself on his mercy and promise him a vote in perpetuity. Maybe that is why the public sector does not provide answers; officials do not want to compete with the minister's clinic! I have attended meetings where senior civil servants have argued against simplifying various processes and procedures. I could never decide whether this reflected a desire to maintain employment at artificially high levels or to keep the confusion going so that ministers would be in a position to do more favours at their clinics. It could also have been to the result of an innate conservatism – or some combination of all three reasons.

Questionable Structures

The Irish public sector has had basically the same structure for a very long time, before, during and after the Celtic Tiger. There are the same fifteen departments of state, more or less, but with a much larger number of quangos reporting to them. There are an amazing 700 different grades in the civil service, ranging from clerical officer to veterinary inspector, from assistant principal to map reader. Such a diverse grading structure obviously creates administrative difficulties and associated costs. Wasn't it General de Gaulle who said it was impossible to run a country that produced 400 different cheeses?

There is ample scope for personal animosities, especially where a quango feels that it can bypass a career civil servant and go straight to the minister. I have had personal experience of extraordinarily difficult situations which had to do with status, access to the minister, feelings of insecurity and so on, but nothing whatever to do with the actual job of work. In many cases, the work can be sabotaged by people with grievances and thin skins. It may be the case that personal grievances and insecurities are more prevalent in the public sector. In the private sector there are bigger worries, like the loss of one's job.

As long ago as 1970, the Devlin Commission suggested that each government department should have a small cadre of policy-makers at the top, called an *aireacht*.[8] The civil service fought against this proposal. They did not want a group of philosopher kings telling them what to do. Ironically, something approaching the hated *aireacht* model actually evolved *faute de mieux*. As more and more practical activities were outsourced to state-sponsored bodies and quangos, the departments of state had less to do and were forced to turn to policy-making, an activity for which they never had much time. Health is the classic example. The Health Service Executive, with its staff of 111,000, does all the work; they deliver the health service. The Department of Health 'does the policy', not because it wants to, but because that is the best rationalisation for its continued existence. Over 500 people are employed in the department, whereas a dozen should be more than enough to come up with policy initiatives. But the basic problem hasn't gone away – that is, the enmity between the 'doers' and the so-called 'policy-makers'. The latter feel superior and demand frequent reports from the executive arm which has to deal with the flak. We have seen HSE officers on television batting on very sticky wickets and often being humiliated. When have we ever seen a policy guru from the Department of Health? Never. How does that make the HSE feel? Could anyone invent a more toxic or demoralising system?

Other government departments seem over-staffed. The Department of Agriculture, Food and Fisheries employs almost 4,300 people. Since agriculture now accounts for just 2 per cent of GNP, surely this is disproportionate? The Courts Service has over 1,100 staff, while the Department of Justice employs 4,608, in addition to 14,000 gardaí. The Department of Education and Science has 1,600 people, in addition to 90,000 teachers. The Department of Foreign Affairs employs some 1,300 people and has 60 fully staffed embassies abroad. It would be interesting to know what value for money the 40 or so smaller embassies yield, and, indeed, the consulates.

The Department of Social and Family Affairs has 4,500 staff while the Revenue Commissioners has a colossal 6,660. There is little doubt that there is ample scope for economies of scale and for centralising functions such as personnel and IT. When organisations are overstaffed and poorly organised, morale suffers because the work is less challenging and also because the genuinely busy staff cannot understand how or why the slackers are tolerated or why they get away with so much casual sick leave.

The tendency to over-staff is in-built. In many instances a manager will increase the number of permanent staff to cope with work-peaks, which may crop up only once or twice a year. Having 'fat' in the system is a comfort to most managers.

Promotion sometimes depends on the number of staff reporting to the manager. I recall one situation where an organisational restructuring left one senior person with less staff than before. He was convinced that he was being 'shafted', even though he had higher-order responsibilities. He lost no time in rebuilding his 'empire'.

Miscellaneous Reasons

There are other reasons for poor public sector performance. These range from loss of vocational commitment (teachers, nurses) to the rapid spread of part-time working, from empire-building as a means to promotion to a growing defensive posture. The last was triggered in large part by the shock of transparency and of the tribunals of inquiry. Civil servants commit much less to paper nowadays and that which is put on file is done in order to cover one's flanks. When transparency was at its height in the 1990s, civil servants had to hand over their diaries as well as official files. The former was potentially embarrassing because of the practice of using shorthand and nicknames. One diary entry I heard of was, 'Meet bogmen at 4.00 pm'.

The Official Secrets Act, 1963 is draconian and instils a degree of fear in the minds of many civil servants. This is one reason why an extraordinarily high number of inefficient practices are kept out of the public eye. Even if a whistleblower's charter were introduced, it might not change the deep-seated desire for secrecy – and perceived loyalty to one's organisation.

To a large degree the prevailing management style is a punitive one. One senior civil servant observed that if he praised his staff, they would 'start getting above themselves and might even look for more money'. Other senior people took the view that the staff had trade unions to look after their interests and that was the end of the matter. Praising staff might merely serve to make the unions'even more demanding.

Ireland's public sector is out of touch with ordinary people. Surprisingly, this seems to be true of the politicians as well. Hence, the defeat of the Lisbon Treaty in the summer of 2008, despite the endorsement of all the major political parties. Another example relates to the agency in charge of road safety, which regularly puts out horrendous television ads about car crashes. These very graphic ads may have some impact on a small proportion of the driving public, but they are counter-productive when it comes to many young men who would regard the depicted horrors as a further challenge to prove their masculinity. Similarly, RTÉ itself has spent years trying the make 'spongers' feel guilty about not paying their television licences. Does anyone seriously believe that in a land of offshore accounts and tax evasion at the highest levels in society, anyone would feel guilty about not buying a TV licence? These and other public service ads indicate a poor understanding of the Irish psyche.

Mention has been made of awkward relations between public bodies and their parent departments. But there are other situations *within* the same organisation where relations between people can be less than cooperative. The average public sector hospital is a case in point. Consultants do not take orders from administrators. Many nurses do not get along with consultants; the fact that nurses now have degrees does not alter the situation. Junior hospital doctors are often badly treated by nurses, consultants and administrators. When these young doctors eventually become consultants, they will have lost most of the idealism and sense of vocation that led them into the profession in the first place. The cycle will repeat itself. One could not design a worse system.

The public sector is rarely proactive, but it can respond well to a crisis, especially where public officials' careers might be in jeopardy. Thus, during the financial crisis of late 2008 a huge state guarantee for banks of €450 billion was hammered out over the course of a few days. The situation should never have been allowed to reach that meltdown stage, but the ability to respond quickly in a crisis is not entirely lacking. This is a national characteristic. In sporting parlance, we are good in defence but don't often push forward to score goals.

It is a truism that public monopolies often become inefficient because there is no competition to keep them on their toes. Many of the staff who work for Dublin Bus and Iarnrod Éireann have very little regard for their passengers. Late arrivals, cancellations and overcrowding are par for the course. In many cases the staff displays scant commitment to their employers either. Some years ago the staff at the DART station in Lansdowne Road used to have a tea break in the signal box at 6.00 p.m. Passengers who arrived between 6.00 p.m. and 6.30 p.m. could usually travel free because the ticket sellers and checkers were enjoying their break and had no interest in the crowd of freeloaders who used to arrive deliberately at that time. No doubt, this was replicated at other stations. Some private-sector buses are at last providing a modicum of competition. In fact, one of the most important developments in the transport sector in the past 40 years is the Patton Flyer, a coach that ran from Dalkey to the airport and back. So successful was this private sector initiative that the government refused to grant the owners a licence! The company went out of business in August 2010.

Finally, the notion of excellence seems to have disappeared, along with the concept of the national interest. The degree to which RTÉ television copies other countries' programmes instead of 'inventing' its own is scarcely credible. We have all the 'big brother' derivatives, *Who Wants to be a Millionaire? Dragons' Den, The Apprentice*, soap operas and so on. Hardly anything is original. Irish radio, on the other hand, is extremely good because we have talented broadcasters, fewer administrators and lower costs.

We cannot leave this chapter without examining the art of politics in Ireland; it is a major part of the public sector. Many of the characteristics mentioned above apply equally to politicians, but there are some additional ones that should be mentioned.

Politics

Emphasis on the Local

As has been said, all politics is local, but this is especially true in Ireland. Even senior politicians put local concerns ahead of national ones. The Shannon stopover was a case in point. Local hospitals and post offices frequently absorb a high proportion of a legislator's time. Some of the best ministers in this country – Justin Keating, John Kelly, Alan Dukes – paid a price because they devoted too much attention to their national duties and not enough to their constituencies. Political scientists tend to the view that this emphasis on local matters is a product of the multi-seat constituency and public relations. Local people are also loyal to their representative, even if he or she has become involved in a national scandal. Voters usually put local matters far ahead of national ones. They do not believe in trickle-down. What's good for Dublin, especially Dublin 4, is, by definition, bad for the rest of the country.

Undue emphasis on the local has cost us dearly. Failure to implement the excellent policy-concept of growth poles put forward by Buchanan[9] over forty years ago was a serious loss to the nation. That idea was years ahead of its time and it anticipated the industrial cluster strategy associated with Harvard Business School's Michael Porter. Today the slow pace of developing centres of excellence in the health service is also extremely costly. Sometimes it seems as if mediocrity is perfectly acceptable as long as it is local mediocrity.

Emphasis on the Short Term

Politicians usually do not look beyond the next election. Losing an election for an Irish politician is much more upsetting than losing a job. In a small community it means loss of face, prestige and self-validation. There is the added hurt of knowing the person who has taken your seat.

Personality Quirks

Very often the people who go into politics seem to need the reassurance of the crowd, in much the same way that actors need applause. Ireland probably has more than its fair share of insecure people, but when they enter politics it is too much to expect strong decision-making. There is probably a higher proportion of people-pleasers and approval-addicts in politics than in most other professions. It is no coincidence that Ireland tends to have populist governments. Sometimes social partnership is put across as being a form of consensus-building, and of course it should be. But it is also a mechanism whereby politicians can find out what the line of least resistance is. Kite-flying, usually based on leaks, is another method used to establish what way the wind is blowing.

Ability

Our system and tradition are designed to produce politicians who are popular rather than able. This is not too bad when the economy is performing well but when it falters, then good, well-conceived policies are hard to come by. Policy advisors find it easy to satisfy a minister who is not too demanding. A mediocre minister, who may have no deep knowledge of his portfolio, will tend to be more interested in hype and spin than in substantive policies which, by definition, will upset the status quo. He will tend to surround himself with PR people and constituency workers. Even if he has good policy advisors, they may be demoralised by the fact that he listens more to his public relations consultants.

Political appointments undermine ability. People are appointed to boards of important state bodies because they have done favours for politicians or are their friends. Such appointments are overt and are not regarded in any way as inappropriate by the opposition parties. Unfortunately, these appointments serve to embed mediocrity and to demoralise professional people. I know of one political appointee who sits on over 12 different boards!

Because of the banking crisis, the financial regulator had to take early retirement. No doubt, he could have done a better job. The fact remains, however, that he was appointed by an authority that was nominated by the government. None of the political appointees had experience of bank regulation. The approach adopted was one of light regulation. It is more than likely that this approach was one that suited the government because of its affinity with property speculators and builders. While the financial regulator did the honourable thing, there was absolutely no question of the authority that had appointed him following suit! It would be hard to invent a system more certain to fail. The tragedy is that no politician of any party sees how disastrous this system is.

Lack of Political Debate

While opposition parties occasionally seem to mount attacks on government policies, it is probably fair to say that these are usually half-hearted. In other words, the political class sticks together; no one rocks the boat alarmingly. There seems to be a tacit understanding not to engage in really aggressive debate. One example of this is that shadow spokesmen never ask ministers technical questions in the Dáil or on television. No one wants to embarrass a minister because of the principle, 'There but for the grace of God go I'. It is almost a form of collusion.

Opposition parties lack passion. They go through leader's question time in the Dáil by rote and with a boring, and tribal, predictability. Issues are raised and then forgotten about. It is extraordinary that the one individual who showed real passion about the health sector in Ireland was Brendan Gleeson, an actor, not a politician. That electrifying moment, on the *Late Late Show*, gave rise to a movie later on. It was called *The Tiger's Tail*, written and directed by John Boorman, and it raised important questions about the Celtic Tiger.

In the run-up to the two Lisbon Treaty referenda, all the main parties (with the exception of Sinn Féin) were in favour and all lobbied hard for a 'yes' vote. The 'no' side was dominated by a new, apolitical movement, Libertas. It was interesting to note that Libertas was attacked from all sides by the conventional political parties. It was accused of dishonesty and conspiracy – charges that political parties would not lay against each other. They joined forces to keep out a new organisation. Their immune systems combined to repel the invading organism. The pity is that we really do need fresh blood in politics.

One reason for the lack of debate is that all the different parties are clustered around the centre of the political spectrum. The failure of the Progressive Democrats has increased this clustering effect since that party had been right of centre. Hence there is no real political debate. Indeed, before the general election in 2007, there was no discussion about the economy, even though it was evident to several economists that a severe recession was imminent. Even now there is little real debate about the jobs crisis. Disproportionate time is devoted to political resignations, for example those of John O'Donoghue, Willie O'Dea and Trevor Sargent – as if these made any significant difference to the state of the nation.

The government took credit for the Celtic Tiger 'miracle'. What was even more remarkable was that few, if any, opposition politicians questioned this claim.

Lobby Groups and Legislation

One often hears the view that politicians should spend more time in the Dáil putting through legislation, rather than 'nursing' their constituencies and pressing the flesh. There is much truth in this view, but it must be acknowledged that the process of passing laws in Ireland is far from ideal. Suppose it is decided to put through a bill to protect consumers. Civil servants and legal draftsmen get to work. The civil servants of the department sponsoring the legislation have the high ground. The draft sent to the Dáil is largely the work of bureaucrats, not politicians. Many TDs are lobbied by vested interests, which engage lawyers for the purpose. There is every possibility that by the time the law is passed, it will be so watered down and full of loopholes as to be practically useless, or it may reflect the views of vested interests to an undue extent.

Then there is the question of implementation. We have many laws that are rarely implemented. These include laws relating to white-collar crime, corporate reporting requirements, health and safety, abortion, smoking, litter, ill-treatment of protected buildings, non-residency for tax purposes and many more. No prosecutions were ever taken under the exchange-control legislation because of doubts about its constitutionality. Consequently, the notion that politicians make good laws and improve society is a little detached from reality. The legislation introduced in July 2010 relating to stag-hunting and puppy-farming was widely regarded as 'trophy legislation' to satisfy the Green Party. Irish legislators have never been benchmarked against lawmakers in other countries.

Economic Policy

We have seen how economic policy is severely circumscribed in Ireland. There is very little the government can do apart from trying to balance the books. But even here strong 'advice' comes from the mandarins of Brussels, who are most anxious that Ireland adheres to *their* fiscal rules; they do not concern themselves with any deflationary effects on the Irish economy. The government tried to make the social partners see sense regarding pay cuts in the public sector, and this was the rock that social partnership foundered on. The bail-out of the banking system played spectacularly into the hands of the unions. It is hard to see the process of fiscal adjustment continuing beyond the 2010 budget. Adjustment-fatigue is likely to set in as the government stares into the void of political extinction, and if civil unrest scares away foreign direct investment.

Concluding Comments

In summary, the public sector (including government) is not qualitatively less efficient than the private sector, since both are staffed primarily by Irish people. We are talking about differences of degree, bearing in mind that the private sector has the major advantage of highly efficient multinational companies. Since the public sector also mainly provides services, there is less scope for productivity increases based on technology.[10]

By comparison with other countries, the Irish public sector is less accountable and less innovative. One could make the argument that the Celtic Tiger, though predicted by the ESRI, caught the public sector unawares. Forecasts of infrastructural needs were woefully inadequate, as was the delivery.

Pay, pensions and job security are somewhat better in the public sector and this is a persistent irritant to the private sector where jobs are being lost every day in the recession, and where wages are being cut. So far the government has been unable to mediate properly between these two groups, and the continuing tension could be another source of civil unrest.

Can the public sector be brought up to speed and redesigned to suit the needs of a modern economy in the twenty-first century? Can it learn from its mistakes? Would it improve if the quality of government improved? The fact that the 2008 report by the OECD[11] was vetted by senior civil servants is not encouraging. Neither is the fact that public sector reform was not dealt with in the 2009 or 2010 budgets. During emergency pay talks just before the budget of 2010, the unions seemed well disposed to public sector reform in exchange for concessions on the pay front. Many commentators thought this odd since the award of benchmarking pay awards some years previously had also been predicated on reform. In any event, the talks collapsed and it seems that public sector reform, whether real or imaginary, has slipped from the agenda. There is a remote possibility of the Croke Park agreement resulting in some reforms, but these are likely to be cosmetic.

Future governments may have no choice but to accelerate programmes of privatisation and public-private partnerships. This seems a pity since these arrangements are far from being a panacea and may give rise to higher costs and over-billing. In the absence of genuine public sector reform, however, there may be no alternative.

6

PASSIVE CONSUMERS

'He's not much of a consumer; he still has his commun-
ion money.' – Overheard on a train

As noted earlier, consumer spending accounts for 50 per cent of GDP in Ireland, and is the largest item on the demand side of the economy. So if it grows fairly rapidly, it is likely that the economy will also grow rapidly, at least in the short term.

Theory tells us that people will consume more if they have higher incomes, if interest rates are low and they are not already too indebted. They may also consume more if their stock of wealth has grown. For example, if houses or equities rise in value, consumers will feel better off, even if it's not directly reflected in their income. Some theories of consumption include confidence factors and one in particular employs the notion of permanent income. What this means is that consumers may not just take the present year's income into account, but will try to figure out what their lifetime income is likely to be before they make large purchases.

If, for example, a budget puts more money into the pockets of consumers, it is possible that they may not rush out to spend it. They may, instead, reflect on how subsequent budgets are likely to affect their long-term (permanent) income. If they think they will have to pay higher taxes in later years, they may decide to save rather than spend. Now that the government has taken money out of the pockets of consumers, it is unlikely that the converse will hold, that is, that consumers will spend as much as ever because they realise that there will be less borrowing and taxation in the future. That carries theory too far. The fact is that consumers have less money to spend and they are also heavily in debt. Therefore, the budgets of 2009 and 2010 will probably have deflationary effects.

Some economists argue that consumption is the only economic activity that provides utility. If a person saves and invests, he does not derive any welfare or utility from such a transaction until the investment generates income which is eventually used for consumption. As we noted earlier, this is quite a restricted view of welfare. Many people derive satisfaction from saving money to leave to their families, for example.

At low levels of income, people can afford only the staples of life – food, clothing and shelter. It is usually at much higher income levels that the consumption of luxury goods and services comes into play. Many types of luxuries fall into the category of 'conspicuous consumption', that is, people like to be seen in large cars or in posh hotels. Theory says that the consumer knows best. If someone spends a fortune on a designer handbag, it is 'worth' the money to the consumer, regardless of what anyone else might think. A Hollywood starlet once remarked that anyone who thought consumption did not bring happiness simply did not know where to go shopping. Again, we can see the assumption of rational behaviour making its dubious presence felt. Consumer spending must always maximise utility; no one can second guess the market by advocating a more responsible, or less frivolous, pattern of consumption.

We can say with some certainty that consumption beyond a certain point runs into diminishing returns. The obvious example is food. If we eat too much rich food, we will have to pay the consequences. If we have five bathrooms in our houses, the utility we get from the fifth one is much less than that which we get from the first. This is also known as the declining marginal utility of income. In other words, if a banker, say, earns 800 times the average industrial wage – the situation in the US before the banking fiasco – it does not follow that they are 800 times better off than the average citizen. In utility terms, they may be only two or three times better off. We see examples of this every day on our congested roads. The person in the 5-litre Mercedes is also stuck in the traffic jam; the extra power of the car is useless. Maybe the driver has a better sound system, but that is the extent of the additional utility. The declining marginal utility of income is an important point to bear in mind for people concerned with equity. Part of inequality is more apparent than real.

This has important implications for policy. If a government decided to impose a high marginal tax rate on the very highest income earners, it might not reduce their welfare by very much. The opposite side of this coin is that if the fruits of such a tax were allocated to people on very low incomes, it could make a huge difference to their welfare. Therefore there is merit in reallocating income from the very top to the very bottom. Such a redistribution would result in improvements in general welfare. The situation becomes more fuzzy and indeterminate in the middle ranges of income. There is not much point in taking money away from a person earning €70,000 a year and giving it to someone earning €50,000 a year.

Maybe the best things in life are not free, but many of the good things are: fresh air, beautiful scenery, public parks, museums and art galleries. Sex is usually free and, according to an

Italian proverb, 'bed is the poor man's opera'. There are also products that are important to us but which are still very inexpensive. Tea is an example. A poor person may derive much the same utility from a nice cup of tea as a millionaire from a glass of Mouton Rothschild 79.

The Celtic Tiger saw an end to absolute poverty in Ireland, but, according to the ESRI, there is still a problem of persistent relative poverty. It is to be hoped that absolute poverty does not re-emerge in the present recession. Unfortunately, there are some signs of this happening – queues for food parcels, vegetable-growing on allotments, increased sales of cheaper foods, including 'white' mince, whiting and custard.

As we saw in Chapter 2, GDP in Ireland was about €200 billion in 2009. Of this total, consumer spending came to about €100 billion, or roughly 50 per cent. What do people spend their money on? Table 3 gives the details for 1999/2000 and for 2004/2005:

*Table 3: **What Irish Consumers Spend On** (% Shares)*

Item	1999/2000	2004/2005
Food	20.4	18.1
Clothing and Footwear	6.1	5.4
Alcohol and Tobacco	7.6	6.0
Fuel and Light	3.7	3.9
Housing	9.6	12.0
Housing Non-durables	2.5	2.2
Housing Durables	4.6	4.5
Miscellaneous Goods	3.4	3.0
Transport	16.4	15.6
Services and Other	25.7	29.2
All Items	100	100

Note: In 2004/2005 the average household income was about €1,000 per week (before income tax) and the average consumer spending was €787 per week. The expenditure was in the proportions shown in the table. Thus, for example, 18.1 per cent of €787 (or €142) was spent on food each week on average in 2004/2005.

We now spend about 18 per cent of our total household income on food, and although this figure is down on the level of a few years earlier, it is still fairly high for a 'wealthy' country. The fall in the share of spending on alcohol and tobacco is to be welcomed. Of note too is the rise in housing, which reflects the increase in house prices and rents.

We now spend almost 30 per cent of household income on services. Many luxury items appear under this heading: meals outside the home, holidays, cinema and theatre, pop concerts. This may also reflect the tendency for prices of services to increase relatively quickly because of the high labour content of most services. The recession is likely to hit this category of spending fairly hard.

Although not shown in Table 3, household spending on education comes to about 2 per cent – only about a third of what we spend on alcohol and tobacco. This is mainly because governments have decided to provide education more or less free of charge, even to those who can well afford to pay for it.

Another interesting point is that if we took the insurance elements out of the above headings and added them together, we would find that we spend about 5 per cent of total household income on insurance of one form or another – house, car, life, and medical. Is insurance too expensive or are we a very insecure society? Probably both.

The snippets of theory and statistics discussed above do not, however, say a great deal about the motivation of consumers in general or of Irish consumers in particular. What kind of consumer values have we acquired from history and culture?

Age

The first point to note is that a young population tends to spend more than an ageing one because young people have to acquire homes and furnishings. When they have children, they have to spend on food and clothing, school and university charges, health insurance, and so on. Older people do not have such expenditure needs and if they have to save for a pension, they will tend to consume very little indeed. This was one of the main reasons why Japan was in recession for most of the 1990s, 'the lost decade'. Ireland has a relatively young age profile and so consumption tends to be quite buoyant in normal times, that is, when there is no recession. The costs of nursing homes, however, are growing very quickly from an already high base. The correlation between age and low consumption may thus be weakened in the future.

Gender

Most decisions about consumer spending are made by women – 80 per cent in the US and Ireland is likely to be about the same. Most women enjoy shopping and regard it as 'retail therapy', whereas most men hate it. Women may sometimes shop on impulse, but they also look for value for money. Irish women will shop anywhere there is variety and good value, whether it is Belfast, London or New York. Men, when they have to shop, just want to get in and out of the nearest store as quickly as possible. There is no impulse shopping, not much comparing of prices, and no window-shopping. Men are not particularly interested in variety or keeping up with fashion trends. Gender differences are thrown into stark relief where shopping is concerned.

There are other groups of people who have different consuming passions and preferences, reflecting cultural differences. The Travelling community, for example, spends very large sums of money on weddings, on funerals and on ornately carved headstones. The settled community has a completely different set of priorities. While the consumption of cocaine cuts across different groups, the preference for heroin seems to be largely restricted to low-income, inner city groups.

Understanding age and sexual differences is important not only for retailers but also for policy-makers. A colleague once observed that the solution to the lack of consumer spending in Japan would have been a subsidised trip for Irishwomen to Tokyo for a couple of weeks. The same colleague, however, also suggested that women operate mainly on the expenditure side of the economy (see Chapter 2), while men tend to operate more on the output side. He went a bit far by arguing that women were the inflationary principle, while men represented productivity!

Historical Influences

Historically, Irish people avoided frivolity in consumption. Indeed, they were highly motivated to save for a rainy day. This was partly owing to the influence of religion – there would always be a day of reckoning around the corner. We were not meant to consume much on this earth in case that meant fewer jewels in the eternal crown. In fact, it was a virtue to mortify the flesh – hence the Lenten emphasis on giving up things, instead of doing something positive.

The dislike of frivolity was also because of the fact that most of us have an agricultural background, if we go back far enough. In the first place, farming was a basic natural activity in which the frivolous had no place. But, more importantly, agriculture was always unpredictable because it was largely influenced by weather. Hence, farmers always tried to put something by in case bad weather would ruin the harvest. A history of chop-and-change government policies related to agriculture added to the unpredictability.

For many years farmers were net savers and it was the urban-dwellers who borrowed for their businesses and for the purchase of consumer durables. Not long after Ireland joined the European Economic Community in 1973, the situation changed. Younger farmers began to borrow, especially for dairying which was capital-intensive. But in general the tendency to save is still fairly strong in Irish people and, despite the high levels of consumption reached during the Celtic Tiger period, the household savings ratio is relatively high in Ireland. The average household saves about 8 per cent of its income at any given time. It rose to over 10 per cent in 2009/2010 because people were afraid to spend in the recession.

This is in contrast to the position in the US economy where household saving is hardly ever much above zero and is sometimes negative. On average, every American has six credit cards. There is some evidence to suggest that people do not regard plastic as real money and are inclined to spend more than they would if credit cards did not exist. People often console themselves after a large purchase with a credit card by saying something like, 'It's OK. American Express is paying'.

It is worth noting that in China, still a poor country, the household savings rate is a staggering 20 per cent. It rises to 50 per cent if you add in the savings of businesses and government. In China, saving is seen as a patriotic duty. It is also noteworthy that there is only one credit card per 100 Chinese adults. This clearly demonstrates that consumption and saving behaviour can vary between different countries and cultures. Because China lends a large part of its savings to the US government, many Americans can spend more than they earn.

Of course, in recessions, savings ratios tend to rise for precautionary reasons, such as the risk of losing one's job. The need to make provision for old age is another powerful stimulus to saving, though in most countries not powerful enough.

The credit card culture is much more embedded in the United States and, while many Irish consumers are now heavily indebted to the banks, this is mainly because of mortgage borrowing and, on average, the household savings ratio is still quite high in Ireland. Nevertheless, it was much higher fifteen years ago, about 17 per cent, and there is always the possibility that people might desire to return to such a 'safe' comfort level. This has implications for policy. If the government tried to stimulate consumer spending by lowering income tax, for example, it might find that the windfall gains were put into savings instead of into consumption. This is a good illustration of why the government needs to understand people if policy is to be correctly designed.

After 13 years of continuous rapid growth from 1995 to 2007 it seemed likely that Irish consumers might go the way of their American counterparts. Confidence had grown to the point where there was no fear of a rainy day. Consumption grew fast during the Celtic Tiger years and even in the period after 2001. The recession that began in 2008 caused a slow-down in consumer spending, but this was mainly the result of the loss of jobs and reduced disposable income. One cannot say yet whether or not it marked a fundamental change from consumption to saving. If the habit of thrift has re-emerged, it may be no bad thing because in the long run saving is important for sustainable growth. Nevertheless, a fall in consumption could depress economic activity in the short term.

Exploitation of Consumers

There is little doubt that Irish consumers have been gouged by producers and retailers over the years and they have not been defended adequately by themselves or by the government. Profit margins, as we discover time and time again, are extremely high in Ireland and every opportunity is taken to extract more and more from the consumer.

Consumers are manipulated by advertising and by product and price discrimination. It has been discovered that consumers tend to value things on a relative basis. So, for example, it will 'pay' a restaurant to put a very expensive dish on the menu even if no one orders it. This is because the customers will tend to use that price as a relative benchmark, and it has been found that many will choose the second most expensive dish, which is also overpriced! A similar gimmick is the 'placebo' effect. This is based on the tendency for consumers to regard a more expensive product as better than a cheaper one. This is especially true in relation to medicines and fashion items. A manufacturer once told me that he tried to place his products in an upmarket store. He was turned down because his prices were not high enough. He replied that he could easily fix that! Such idiocy occurred during the Celtic Tiger period.

Manipulation of customers is very easy for producers and service-providers because in most cases the buyers do not have nearly as much information about the goods and services in question. This 'information asymmetry' problem is so subtle and pervasive that no regulator would be able to weed it out. Consumers should exercise constant vigilance and vote with their feet. By going north of the border to shop, consumers forced Tesco to reduce its prices in the Republic. This is a marvellous example of consumer power in action, but, unfortunately, it is all too rare.

Until 2006 there was a Groceries Order that prevented below-cost selling for the previous two decades. The rationalisation was that a retailer or supplier could drive competitors out of business, become a monopoly and then really exploit the consumer. This was disingenuous because if below-cost selling ever did give rise to monopoly power, then the Competition Authority would have to rectify the situation. This was yet another example of how the government always favours producers over consumers.

Another example in the early years of Ireland's EU membership was the policy of dear food, which was designed to help farmers, who paid very little tax, at the expense of the buying public who paid a lot of tax. This was in stark contrast to the cheap food policy in the UK, which was designed to benefit consumers.

Home Ownership Again

In earlier chapters we discussed the desire of the Irish to own their own homes, almost regardless of cost, and the figure for home ownership is around 80 per cent, one of the highest in the world. The idea of paying rent, 'dead money', does not appeal to us and presumably it must bear some relationship to our colonial past. Even if statisticians classify houses as investment goods, there is no doubt that home-owners regard them as consumer goods – durable ones it is to be hoped. Irish families become very attached to their homes and neighbourhoods.

Some years ago RTÉ showed an eviction scene. A bank had foreclosed on a property in County Donegal and we saw bailiffs breaking down the door with sledgehammers. Many viewers were shocked. The rights and wrongs of the situation did not matter; the image of the eviction struck a sensitive chord in people.[1] That is why banks are reluctant to foreclose. This is quite unlike other countries. In the US, for example, foreclosures are now an everyday occurrence, following the sub-prime disaster, and property speculators are buying up these properties for 20 cents on the dollar or even less.

Keeping Up with the Joneses

One of the main motivations behind consumption is that of relativities or 'keeping up with the Joneses'. In relation to disposable income, the desire to protect relativities is usually worked out in the context of social partnership. But consumers also tend to watch each other to make sure they are not falling behind their chosen peer group. It is not a uniquely Irish phenomenon. The Greeks say that 'the potter watches the potter'. The closest Irish analogue is, 'the beetle recognises another beetle'. In a small island society we watch each other like hawks. No doubt, this does influence consumer spending. Indeed, many advertisements for consumer products use the 'hook' of peer groups.

If there were a clearly demarcated upper class in Ireland, we probably would not try to emulate its incomes or patterns of consumption. But since we all come from the same seed and breed, we do tend to feel reduced if our 'equals' get one jump ahead. Gore Vidal once observed that 'when a friend succeeded, a little something in him died'. Maybe we're not as envious as that but we do try to keep up, while of course avoiding the impression that we're 'getting ahead of ourselves'. In the good years when taxi drivers would talk about their villas in Spain and Bulgaria, it was hard not to start doing some mental arithmetic in the back of the cab. Peer pressure in consuming has a lot to do with our perceptions of where we fit into society.

There were always certain goods that were 'markers' or status symbols. I remember when dishwashers and microwave ovens fell into that category. Foreign holidays filled the bill for a while, before airline competition made international travel affordable for most people. Nowadays, we have Mercedes cars, SUVs, designer clothes and big houses. I recently came across a magazine which advised Irish women about how to deal with their gardeners, nannies and chauffeurs. One of the great puzzles relates to cosmetic surgery. One might have thought that surgery of this sort would be kept secret, but a surprising number of women have no difficulty in admitting to having had various procedures.² The conspicuous consumption aspect seems to have taken over from vanity.

During the Celtic Tiger years, keeping up with the Joneses forced a lot of people into debt. But the associated spending kept the economy going even after the foreign direct investment and export performance slowed down. Consumer spending was also facilitated by second mortgages on property that had shot up in value, and by tailor-made consumer loans actively marketed by the banks. Indeed, many young people who could not get on to the property ladder found themselves with large discretionary incomes, especially if they lived with their parents, and it was common to see these young people driving around in sports cars and dining in the best restaurants.

Excessive Consumption

There was a danger in the high growth years that we could become a nation of consumers, along the American model. But what works for America would not necessarily work here. The main reason why high mass consumption in Ireland might have been risky is because we depend so much on foreign industry. It might be all right for a nation to consume all its own output. But for a nation to consume all its own output, as well as the output of foreign industry lured here by low tax rates, could be deemed to be excessive – and probably unsustainable. We could hardly depend indefinitely on foreign industry to keep us in the style to which we had become accustomed. The present recession has forced that lesson on us in no uncertain terms.

A large part of what we consumed was in a sense what others had produced. No moral point is being made here. It is arguable that this was a brilliant policy and the essence of capitalism, that is, minimise effort by attracting foreign direct investment, and maximise utility via consumption. This policy has lasted for about fifty years, so does it really have to come to an end?

The tragedy of economics is that many policies contain the seeds of their own eventual destruction. By creating a gap between consumption and production in Ireland, we are also creating unrealistic expectations. It is these psychological factors that tend to undermine the original policy. We come to believe that we are perfectly entitled to high mass consumption and a good lifestyle, even though we have not put in the effort that would be expected in a more normal economy. We have not done the research or trained our own entrepreneurs and marketing experts; we have not put up our own risk capital. There is something of the fool's paradise about this. Unfortunately, no government is ever going to tell the truth about the core vulnerability of one of its major policies. Instead, governments pretend they brought us the good life. The average person has no way of knowing that we have had it far too easy.

Why should the US stop investing in Ireland? The reasons are given elsewhere, but they include pressure from the EU and from US politicians. And if all that weren't enough, we have become uncompetitive – precisely because we wanted to consume so much and that meant high wages, which we awarded ourselves from the ATM known as 'social partnership'.

The following figures tell the story. Between 1995 and 2008 consumer spending in Ireland grew by over 6 per cent per annum in real terms. The output of Irish-owned manufacturing industry grew by less than 3 per cent per annum. This huge gap was filled by foreign industry based here, and by imports.

Moral Values

Many observers have argued that our years of high mass consumption were characterised by a loss of moral values. This is nothing more than the tired old cliché that consumption is the principal component of materialism which lures us away from the spiritual. There is no evidence for this contention. In many ways this kind of critique comes from 'old money' looking down on 'new money'.

The fact is that money in itself is neutral. If we have more of it, we can decide to spend it on drink and drugs or we can give it to the poor. Money in itself doesn't make us do any of these things. It simply gives us more choice. If a society is immoral to start with, then more money will make it worse, but the converse is also true.

Other commentators claim that the need to meet mortgage repayments has forced women out to work and put children's welfare in jeopardy. Even if this were true, it only proves the point, because if the women had even *more* money, they wouldn't have to go out to work in the first place!

Money does not corrupt. The Celtic Tiger took many people out of absolute poverty and created jobs that allowed more people to lead fulfilling lives. It created a wider range of choice for people. If church attendances fell, it may have more to do with the implosion of the institutional church than to 'materialism'.

There is, however, a wider issue here. The booming economy attracted many thousands of immigrants to our shores and we became a multicultural country in a short space of time. This, combined with post-modern values, meant that the influence of the Catholic Church and its ethos became much more diluted. But that was simply a diminution of orthodoxy, not rampant materialism.

Nevertheless, the free and easy consumption of the last thirteen years may have softened us a little bit, and raised expectations to unrealistic levels. It is to be hoped that we will be strong enough to survive the present severe recession and accept the short-term pain required for the restoration of competitiveness.

Widening the Range of Choice

Many economists believe that increasing the effective range of choice for human beings is the main objective of economic development. Choice can be exercised responsibly or irresponsibly. This depends on the individual's value system; it is not affected by an increase in their income. For many hundreds of years Irish people did not have the luxury of choice and there is little doubt that the ability to exercise choice in the marketplace is a fulfiling experience for many.

I have heard people say how their parents would have loved to have owned a car or a television set or a clothes washer. A hundred years ago the average man spent 20 per cent of his time chopping wood for fuel and the average woman spent about the same proportion of her time washing clothes. The time that has been saved from these chores greatly increases our ability to choose how to live our lives.

At a more micro level, the ability to choose between different goods and services is part of the attraction of consuming. I am reliably informed that Irish women in a restaurant believe that choosing a meal from a menu is half the fun. There is little doubt that a formerly oppressed people will enjoy the act of choosing – and having the wherewithal to execute that choice. In fact, we probably derive more satisfaction from consuming than many other peoples. One of the great disadvantages of the present recession is that this simple pleasure will be denied to many individuals.

Another aspect of choice is that between present and future consumption. Irish people on average would prefer to have a given sum of money now rather than wait for a larger sum in, say, a year. This means that we tend to discount the future at a fairly high rate. To us, a bird in the hand is worth two in the bush. It does not necessarily follow that we will spend all the money today, but we prefer to have it now rather than the promise of more tomorrow. This clearly reflects a degree of uncertainty about the future, perhaps insecurity as well, and a lack of trust.

It is not exactly a Micawber attitude – 'something will turn up'. We are not that optimistic, and tend to believe in Murphy's law. It is more a question of the security of having the money up front and having the power to choose now. We might well save a high proportion of the money, but that will be our choice. Having the money now gives us more control.

Unorthodox Consumer Behaviour – An Example

In the late 1980s Charles Haughey took the advice of his wealthy colleagues who were worried about the possibility of the country going bankrupt and about the IMF taking charge for a few years. The surprising thing was that fiscal retrenchment did not depress the economy. Many commentators feared that it would have precisely that Keynesian effect. Economists in the Central Bank were of the view that it might not, mainly because the private sector would no longer be 'crowded out' by big government.

As a result of fiscal contraction, the average person had less money in their pocket but they had something else which was just as important: confidence. People were relieved that the government was finally stopping the slide into fiscal disaster which would inevitably lead to higher taxes later on. The result was that consumer spending did not fall, but rather the reverse. Hence, the paradox of 'expansionary fiscal contraction' which is sometimes attributed to David Ricardo.[3] Many economists from various parts of the world wrote about this 'paradoxical' behaviour on the part of Irish consumers.

The question which then arose was whether or not Irish consumers would always behave like that. There are no firm answers to that question. My own view is that the Ricardian version probably did dominate the Keynesian one on that occasion. However, I do not believe that we can base a whole new theory of behaviour on one observation. The same response might not happen again. I tend to believe that the Keynesian response would be the correct one about seven times out of ten. In other words, Irish people will tend to spend windfall gains and, if money is taken away from them by higher taxes, they will curtail their spending. As consumers, we tend not to look too far ahead.

If this view is correct, then the government's budgets of 2009 and 2010 were poorly designed. The main emphasis was on trying to reduce the deficit by some €4 billion a year. It might have been better to let the deficit widen, at least to some extent, and finance it from the national pension fund or by borrowing or, indeed, by cutting back on wasteful expenditure by the public sector. By putting more spending power into circulation, consumption might be encouraged and this would keep the economy from going too deeply into recession, especially at a time when prices are falling. The real danger is that a deep recession might make some people, especially entrepreneurs, lose confidence in the future. They might come to believe that the Celtic Tiger was a fluke and that the sustainable growth rate of the Irish economy is low. We could be at a tipping point. A somewhat expansionary budget in 2009 and 2010 might have pulled us back a little from the brink and given us some breathing space. If the Keynesian effect is the dominant one, aggregate demand could be very depressed indeed. We could see negative growth in real GNP of over 12 per cent between 2008 and 2011, and a jump in unemployment to some 14 per cent or more if emigration does not increase. The government is committed to at least two more years of deflationary policy beyond 2011. Despite the difficulties of borrowing on international capital markets, it is strange that the government is not more alert to the serious risk of continuing deflation. In early 2010 consumer spending was still very depressed and imports of consumption (and investment) goods was down on the previous year by an alarming 23 per cent in nominal terms. It is interesting to note that this downside risk of deflation apparently weighed more heavily with George Lee than with the Fine Gael party which tended to side with the government.

Organising Consumers

By comparison with other countries, Irish consumers are not well organised. Over the years, governments have treated consumers badly. No political party has ever made 'consumerism' an issue. There were four pillars involved in social partnership: government, trade unions, employers and representatives of the underprivileged. But consumers per se, that is, as a group with a common purpose, are not represented and have never been invited into the tent of social partnership, and certainly not into that other tent at the Galway Races.

This is strange, given that, potentially, consumers could be the most powerful lobby group of all. Political contributions come mainly from producers, employers and unions. Because of lack of organisation, consumers have never been wooed by political parties. Given the hostile reaction to the 2009 and 2010 budgets, this may be changing; the sleeping giant may be waking up – and not before time.

Irish consumers are far too docile, accepting shoddy merchandise, over-priced meals and other services with a resigned shrug. We are bad at complaining about poor service and inferior, overpriced goods, and do not want to draw attention to ourselves in public places such as restaurants and hotels. Even in recession we meekly accept the fact that a broad range of prices have not been reduced; for example, the fees charged by doctors, dentists and lawyers. We might haggle in a flea market, but not in a shop, and certainly not with 'professional' people. We don't want to 'let ourselves down', as the saying goes. If Oprah Winfrey were analysing Irish consumers, she would undoubtedly say it was all because of low self-esteem. We don't deserve the best.

Some years ago a colleague complained about a meal in a pub – the chicken he had been served was almost raw. He was barred! On another occasion a friend tried to return a bottle of wine which was corked. The waiter refused, saying that there was nothing wrong with the 'bleedin' wine'. Then there was the famous case of a CIE man telling a new recruit he didn't have to worry about a certain individual because he was only a 'fucking passenger'.

As consumers, we have all been conned on this island in one way or another and there is usually almost nothing that can be done about it. No one can afford to go to court, and the various state agencies – for example, the National Consumer Agency and the Financial Services Ombudsman – that are supposed to look after consumer interests are fragmented, riddled with political appointees, and fairly stand-offish.

This isn't bad just for consumers. It is bad for the whole economy because a nation's consumers are really its quality controllers. If Irish companies had to satisfy domestic consumers who were extremely demanding with regard to quality and price, and who were backed up by efficient state agencies, then those companies would have a very good chance of exporting their goods and services around the world. If, however, domestic consumers are not demanding, then it will be difficult for producers of goods and services to break into export markets. It is no coincidence that the most successful economies in the world have the most demanding consumers. American, German and Japanese consumers simply do not accept second-best.

Passing by the Shelbourne Hotel in the summer of 2010, I noticed the commissionaire whistling up a cab for an American couple who had just come out of the hotel. One cab drove up from a nearby rank. The car was seven years old but in reasonable condition. The American man said very loudly to the commissionaire, 'Do you expect us to get into that rust-bucket?' Would any Irish person have said that, especially in a foreign country?

It is worth remembering that over 70 per cent of our total exports come from foreign firms located in Ireland. A very small proportion of exports comes from Irish firms. This is partly because these firms never had to satisfy demanding consumers or achieve high standards of excellence.

The fact that Irish consumers are too docile explains this country's very high rate of indirect taxation. Income tax payers, producers and union members were all looked after in the tent of social partnership before it imploded. The government often reduced income tax in order to broker a pay deal. But then the tax was levied on the consumer, who was not represented in those discussions. That is why VAT is so high in Ireland and also why we have stealth taxes, like Vehicle Registration Tax and stamp duty on house purchases. The Irish consumer takes it all on the chin. The only reason VAT is not even higher is because more Irish consumers would go over the border to shop.

To some extent consumers are their own worst enemies. While some Irish people like to flaunt their consumption, the majority tend to be fairly coy, as if there were a legacy of guilt about the whole exercise. A man of my acquaintance feels guilty about buying himself new socks and on one occasion became faint in the hosiery aisle. In fact where savings are concerned (the other side of the consumer coin), Irish people are coy in the extreme. Very few people talk about their savings and fewer still admit to having any. There has never been a lobby group or even an individual who has argued publicly that banks should offer higher interest rates on deposits. When we had control over interest rates, there was a very powerful debtors' lobby group, always arguing for lower interest rates on loans. But there has never been a representative group of savers, even when the savings were kept onshore! A visitor might be forgiven for believing that no one in Ireland had any savings.

Some Miscellaneous Irrational Behaviours

Why do we keep billions of euro in ordinary deposit accounts earning less than 0.5 per cent interest when, at the stroke of a pen, we could quadruple that rate of return and still have easy access to our funds? We either do not bother to seek information on better financial products or we regard money coming from interest as less valuable than money coming from other sources. In fact, most people suffer from money illusion where savings are concerned – though not wages and salaries. In any case our irrational behaviour has for years made banking a very lucrative activity, until greed and the property bubble met in an icy kiss.

Investors in equities hardly complained in mid-2008 when gilt-edged Irish shares plummeted by 70 per cent and more. Whether people were direct or indirect investors (via pension funds), there was a deafening silence. Perhaps the anger surfaced in other ways, such as demonstrations in the streets, a collapse of Fianna Fáil in the opinion polls, and a marked swing to Labour which is bound to worry the international markets and credit rating agencies.

Although Irish consumers are not on average overly responsive to interest rate changes on savings products, we do respond to other more direct forms of incentive. For example, the Special Savings Investment Account (SSIA) scheme had a very high uptake from the moment it was introduced in 2001. This may not have been owing solely to the higher interest rate offered, but rather to the fact that the government was handing out something for nothing. It was like getting money back from the taxman. That scheme, incidentally, may have been prompted in part by the disastrous privatisation of Eircom. Investors in Eircom did protest because they believed they were conned by the government. The SSIA scheme may well have been an attempt to compensate the middle classes for the losses suffered in the botched privatisation of Eircom.

There are many other irrational forms of consumer behaviour in Ireland. We project our preferences into the future based on our existing tastes, but when the future comes, our tastes might have changed. Or fashions might have changed. Being a 'fashion victim' is irrational – but the phenomenon exists.

When someone consumes a good or service, they derive utility (or welfare) from it. Delayed consumption, therefore, is supposed to cause 'disutility', and that is why we earn interest on savings. It is to compensate us for postponing the pleasure of instant consumption. But this ignores the pleasure of anticipation. Even though the latter may be waning in an era of instant gratification, it probably still exists to some extent.

If we are making a major purchase – a car, say – we won't worry unduly about whether or not we are overcharged by €10. But if we are overcharged by this amount when buying a bicycle, we will be annoyed. This is not rational, as far as most economists are concerned, because the same amount of money is involved in both cases. If our neighbour is overcharged by the same amount, this will lessen our annoyance. This is not rational either!

Irish consumers, especially males, are incensed when a neighbour informs them that they paid too much and that better bargains were available. I know of one man whose wife continues to shop around long after he has made his purchases. Inevitably, she informs him that he has paid too much. This put a strain on the marriage – until he decided to leave all the spending decisions to her. That could, of course, have been her intention all along!

When we are exploited, we tend to feel a sense of personal failure. This might mean that house-owners who now find themselves in negative equity will react badly because they feel cheated, especially in comparison with neighbours who still have positive equity. It is important that government understands the reactions of its citizens because it is these reactions that influence economic events; they also determine whether or not government policies will be successful.

In some countries there is an 'endowment effect', that is, people prefer goods they are used to and tend to put a lower value on newer, replacement goods. Of course, some goods have sentimental value but, that apart, I am not sure if the endowment effect is much in evidence in Ireland. Certainly where house trade-ups are concerned, most people do not seem reluctant to leave the 'old' house behind.

Lowenstein has dealt with the role of emotions, rather than reason, in consumer choice.[4] He takes the example of the infamous head butt by Zinedine Zidane at the end of the 2006 World Cup. The economist would have to argue that in deciding to deliver the head butt, Zidane would have had to weigh up the immediate satisfaction against the longer-term disutility of damaging his own reputation and that of his country. It is highly unlikely that such a calculation was made. The role of visceral emotion does complicate economic theory and introduces a random element into the behaviour of consumers – and indeed of entrepreneurs.

Concluding Comments

Consumers are very important to the health of an economy, and almost as important as entrepreneurs. If consumers lose confidence or suffer a loss of buying power, as is happening now, this can have a major influence on economic growth, especially in the short term.

If foreign consumer demand is buoyant, it will benefit our exports. But it is difficult for entrepreneurs to break into export markets quickly enough to compensate for a fall in domestic demand.

There is probably a satiation level for the consumption of food and certain other goods and services, ranging from hair-cuts to cinema visits, but in general Irish consumers, having shrugged off the caution associated with farming, demonstrated during the Celtic Tiger years that there was no upper limit on demand for luxury goods – large houses, expensive furnishings, fashionable clothes, designer shoes and handbags, foreign holidays, visits to nightclubs, fast cars, SUVs, cosmetic surgery. Declining marginal utility did not apparently curb these high expenditures which were also driven by a desire to 'keep up with the Joneses'.

Maybe some people were too free with their money but there is no evidence that high mass consumption turned us all into amoral materialists. One of the welcome features of growing incomes is that it affords us the ability to choose. This is clearly very important for a people whose forebears were deprived of choice.

Irish consumers depend to an unusually high degree on the output of foreign industry located here, thus allowing us to consume far more than we ourselves produce. The gap between domestic demand and domestic supply does give rise to a sense of easy entitlement, which could cause an imbalance in the economy in the long run. To some extent it might have contributed to the property bubble.

The recession has hit the demand for luxuries hard and many jobs have been lost. Transferring buying power from the very rich to the very poor would yield improvements for society as a whole and would also help to sustain consumption – because the poor have to spend a high proportion of their income on basic consumer goods.

The recession could continue to damage consumer confidence and this might well result in people saving a higher proportion of a lower income. This could deepen and prolong the recession. In the 2009 budgets, and again in 2010, the government did little or nothing to offset this possibility. In fact, the additional taxes and spending cuts could severely undercut consumer spending and hence adversely affect the whole economy. This has to be weighed against the benefits of fiscal rectitude.

Consumers in Ireland should be better organised and there should be more competition to make sure that the prices of consumer goods and services are as low as possible. The nation is full of well-organised lobby groups – all on the production side of the economy. There is no effective lobby group for consumers and they have been badly treated over the years. This is unfair but it is also very bad for the economy because the more demanding consumers become, the more they will act as quality controllers. This is necessary to achieve excellence and to prepare domestic producers for selling abroad.

The behaviour of Irish consumers will exert a major influence on future growth and development.

7

INSECURE WORKERS

'Well, we can't stand around here doing nothing, people will think we're workmen.' – Spike Milligan, *Hitler, My Part in His Downfall*

When our distant forebears worked as hunters and farmers, there was hunger and hardship but no interpersonal angst; this came much later when we had to work for other people, who told us what to do. Not everyone likes being an employee and, as we have seen, work is meant to be a disutility. That is why we get paid a wage or salary. In truth, though, many people actually like their jobs; for many, a job done well is a source of satisfaction and self-validation.

In Ireland, survey data indicate that a high proportion of young people would like to be entrepreneurs, but in truth most of us become employees. The fact that the economy depends so much on foreign direct investment means that many of us can get – or at least could get – good jobs with American multinationals.

Many employees are members of trade unions which provide protection. The unions were vitally important in the Industrial Revolution in nineteenth-century Britain when workers were very badly treated, when children were sent up chimneys as sweeps, and when the educational system refused to teach arithmetic in case the workers could figure out their wages. Nowadays in Ireland, the most unionised employees are those in the public sector – staff who, on the face of it, do not seem to need a great deal of protection. The biggest risk to a private sector worker is losing their job or having to retire on a meagre pension; the biggest risk to a public sector worker is having to accept a pay cut or higher taxes at a time of fiscal stringency.

The so-called 'militancy' of workers varies enormously from country to country. Japan, Germany and Switzerland appear to have few industrial relations problems, whereas countries like Argentina, Mexico, Greece and France seem to lie at the other end of the spectrum. Ireland is somewhere in the middle, though close enough to France. There is little doubt that organisations and institutional arrangements do influence industrial relations, but it is also the case that the country's prevailing 'culture' plays a large part. In Ireland, social partnership was set up largely to avoid industrial relations problems which had been quite serious in the 1960s and 1970s. Unfortunately, social partnership led to a loss of competitiveness which seriously damaged the economy.

Basic Facts

About twenty years ago the labour force in Ireland was just over one million. Of that number, some 13 per cent could not find work. By 2008 the labour force had doubled to over two million and the unemployment rate had fallen to not much more than 4 per cent. This was a remarkable improvement. Unfortunately, the recession has led to a marked deterioration in this situation. In June 2010 there were 453,000 unemployed people on the Live Register, 13.5 per cent of the labour force. Most forecasts indicate a significant deterioration. With recession in the western world it is unlikely that emigration will be the 'safety valve' it was in former years, although it has begun to increase and is expected to reach 120,0000 over the two years 2010 and 2011.

Table 4 sets out the main facts regarding employment and unemployment in Ireland in the period immediately after the Celtic Tiger and before the present recession.

Table 4: Numbers Employed (March–May in 000s)

Sector	2001	2008	% Change
Agriculture, Forestry & Fishing	122.5	121.3	-0.9
Other Production Industries	318.1	286.4	-10.0
Construction	180.0	255.0	42.0
Wholesale & Retail Trade	247.8	310.7	25.4
Hotel & Restaurants	103.8	128.6	23.5
Transport, Storage & Communication	111.1	119.2	7.3
Finance & Other Business Services	217.1	296.3	36.5
Public Administration & Defence	81.3	103.0	27.0
Education	103.8	142.0	36.8
Health	144.0	223.9	55.5
Other Services	92.4	122.1	32.3
Total Employment	1,721.9	2,108.5	22.5
Total Population	3,900.0	4,200.0	8.0
Dependency Ratio	2.26	2.0	–11.5

Even in this short period, the total in employment rose by 22.5 per cent. While the population as a whole also increased (partly as a result of immigration), the dependency ratio continued to fall. In 2001, for example, every worker in employment had to support 1.26 'dependants' – whether old or young or unemployed. By 2008 this had fallen to one 'dependant'. This continued a long downward trend in the dependency ratio. Most economists regard this as a good thing, and indeed many believe this favourable demographic trend was partly responsible for the Celtic Tiger. This is probably correct, though there is not a great deal of evidence to support it. There are many examples of individuals who work extremely hard precisely because they have to support two or more dependants.

We can also see from Table 4 that the growth sectors for employment were health, construction, finance and education. Employment in agriculture continued its secular decline and the category 'other production industries' also experienced a decline; these industries were mainly indigenous Irish manufacturing where competitiveness was eroded vis-à-vis other countries. Employment in construction was bound to fall from its very high level of 255,000. That has contributed to an appalling situation where about a third of all young men are currently unemployed.

It is worth noting the almost universal trend in favour of services of one kind or another, especially financial services, at the expense of older style manufacturing. This trend seems to accord with our preference for computer screens over assembly lines. An important question is how far this trend towards services can continue. Will modern economies end up taking in each other's washing?

Causes of Unemployment

Normally there are two reasons for unemployment. The first is that the economy is not growing quickly enough; hence the demand for labour at the going wage rate is deficient. This is usually referred to as the cyclical cause. The second reason is 'structural', meaning that there is something wrong with the structure of the labour market. Examples include over-generous dole provisions, trade union demarcations and restrictive practices, poor employer rights, and wage agreements which do not reflect productivity.

In the early 1980s both factors were in play – the cyclical and the structural. Around that time I gave a talk to a group of managers from private sector companies, and afterwards took a straw poll. The result was astounding. Not one of them would hire new workers unless it was absolutely necessary. They would look for ways to use machinery and technology instead. 'Machines don't talk back' was one view. Demarcation disputes were the bane of another executive's life. The consensus was that, despite interviewing techniques, there was no guarantee that a new worker would not be a rabble-rouser who could destabilise the existing workforce and bring production to a halt. At the time, nearly any worker who was let go could sue the company and usually be well compensated for unfair dismissal. It was also felt that generous dole payments undermined incentives to work.

The views of those executives were sobering, but fortunately the rising tide of later years had a beneficial effect on such attitudes, and many thousands of jobs were created. At the same time trade union leaders moved much closer to the establishment view of things. Now that we are again in recession – and probably for three to four years – it is to be hoped that such anti-labour attitudes do not surface again. The problem with trade union militancy is that it works for a while but in the longer term it can harden employers' attitudes about creating new jobs.

During the Celtic Tiger years many married women went back to work; individualisation of the income tax code was an added incentive. Child-minding facilities remained problematic and expensive, but female participation in the labour force in Ireland grew rapidly towards EU standards. Flexible working hours and job-sharing became the norm, especially in the public sector. Bringing down the unemployment rate to 4 per cent was a marvellous achievement, especially in the light of large-scale immigration.

Unfortunately, that all changed in 2008, and both unemployment and emigration are continuing to increase in 2010. Cyclical and structural factors are again in evidence. Demand is deficient because of the collapse of the property bubble and of the banking system, and because of recession abroad. Government policy has added a deflationary bias. Social partnership, before it collapsed, had contributed to a loss of competitiveness and to a generous social welfare system. In late 2009, a young woman rang the Joe Duffy show to say that she had been offered a job at €330 a week. She turned it down because, allowing for bus fares and child-minding, she was considerably better off on the dole. Callers rang the show to say she was a 'sponger'. She was nothing of the sort. She was reacting in a perfectly logical way to the incentives provided by government.

Conventional economics does not explain well the persistence of unemployment. According to the basic laws of supply and demand, everyone who wants a job should be able to get one if they lower their wage to a rate that will be acceptable. This is what happens in other 'markets'. Some of the new 'behavioural' economists now incline to the view that the concept of fairness does apply to the labour market, though not to other markets. Employers want to be fair to their workers or at least be seen to be fair. They also want a contented labour force. Since employers cannot always supervise the people who work for them, they reckon that the best way to maintain productivity is to pay fair wages. This, they believe, will help morale and prevent shirking on the job. In the aggregate, this behaviour means that wages will always tend to be higher than those determined solely by the market. Hence, the existence of some involuntary unemployment for most of the time. In other words, there could be more jobs offered at lower wages but it is the employers who decide not to reduce wages to this level. There is some evidence of this in Ireland where American multinational companies pay above the odds to compensate staff for not joining unions.

In a recession there may be some hoarding of labour to start with, but eventually, despite some reduction in wages, there will inevitably be rising unemployment. Many property-related companies have gone bankrupt and have let all their workers go. In Ireland, the unemployment rate could reach 14 per cent by the end of 2011 unless net emigration increases further. There is some kind of contagion effect at work here among employers who want to 'slim down' at the same rate as other employers. Indeed, unemployment tends to feed on itself.

Jobs in the Celtic Tiger Years

It is hard to imagine that only a few years ago the government sent teams abroad to recruit foreign workers, such as computer specialists from India and nurses from the Philippines. The private sector also brought in many Eastern Europeans and Brazilians to work in construction and meat processing respectively. The danger that this increase in labour supply might drive down wages (as it would normally do) was prevented by the government and the unions. Legally, no distinction could be made between locals and immigrants where wages were concerned, though in practice there were several deviations from this rule.

For a while there was a debate about accelerating economic growth to create jobs for immigrants – when we had practically full employment for Irish people. Surely it would be better, so the argument ran, to keep the economy ticking over rather than expanding it aggressively to create jobs for non-nationals. Whatever about the ethics of this view, there were at least two practical counter-arguments.

First, the government had bragging rights about the stellar performance of the economy and of course revenue was flooding into the state coffers without any increase in tax rates. The national debt as a proportion of GNP fell to about 35 per cent in 2006 – one of the lowest in the EU. Second, the notion of asking the Industrial Development Authority to throttle back for a year or two did not make sense. Its high profile would be damaged; there would be no guarantee that when we needed to crank up the IDA again it would have the same good reputation abroad as it had in the past. Development agencies from other countries would have encroached on its turf. In a way, the high growth years, 1995 to 2008, were a treadmill. We could not afford to slow down. It was analogous to the 'bicycle theory' of Japan; if you slow down, you will probably fall off. In Ireland the government finances depended crucially on rapid growth, especially in the property market. Any slowdown was bound to cause a hard landing.

So immigration continued and there is little doubt that the economy prospered (though it may have grown too fast) and that Irish workers broadened their horizons by working alongside people of different nationalities. In fact, one of the enduring legacies of the boom years will be the multicultural experience we all shared. The fact that many skilled people came to our shores for work also did a lot for national confidence.

Labour Productivity

This is usually defined as the volume of output divided by the number of workers. In the high growth years of 1995 to 2008, labour productivity grew rapidly and we convinced ourselves that this reflected our new high-tech economy. In a way it did, but only because of strong inflows of direct investment from the United States. When workers have a lot of horse-power at their elbow, then of course output per head will rise. When that horse-power takes the form of high-speed computers and complex robotics, then productivity can soar. In the US they discovered a similar phenomenon and dubbed it the 'new economy'.[1] Some writers think that Alan Greenspan, Chairman of the US Fed, came to believe that this upward shift in productivity justified the 'irrational exuberance' of speculators that, in an earlier period, had caused him anxiety.[2]

When productivity increases, it is natural that workers will seek higher compensation, even though the driver of productivity is technology rather the work effort per se. One formula that has been proposed is that the fruits of a productivity jump should be shared out in three ways: one-third to the employees, one-third to the entrepreneurs who invested in the technology and took the risks, and one-third to the consumer, who should also benefit from improved productivity, but who seldom does. The free market, alas, rarely produces this equitable result. Indeed, the consumer hardly ever benefits from increased productivity unless there is ferocious competition in the marketplace.

In any case, Ireland's period of high productivity resulted in higher wages (partly because of the collective myopia of the social partners). Irish employers also benefited, but consumers did not get their share. We assumed that high productivity growth was here to stay, but it wasn't and when it began to slow in 2002 we still did not realise that we had been paying ourselves too handsomely. Competitiveness suffered and exports slowed considerably, with the exception of pharmaceutical products.

In the context of social partnership, the government was favourably disposed to the trade unions – far more than the governments of other western democracies – and since the state coffers were overflowing, there seemed to be no budget constraint. The emphasis was on industrial peace (and on political populism), rather than on cost competitiveness. Public sector workers did extremely well out of the so-called 'benchmarking' exercise. Now that recession has struck – and it was entirely predictable – the state is finding it very difficult to pay the high wages of public officials. Indeed, in the budgets of 2009 and 2010 we witnessed crude attempts to raise revenue from the poorest of the poor, rather than tackling the problem of an overpaid and overstaffed bureaucracy.

Pay claims are usually formulated on the basis of cost-of-living increases plus increased productivity. Employees are very much aware of inflation nowadays, and their unions employ economists to analyse all the data relevant to pay. Now that prices are falling, however, it does not follow that nominal wages will also fall. This poses a particular problem in trying to restore competitiveness.

Theory suggests that if unemployment is high, then employees will settle for lower wages. Indeed, Margaret Thatcher always liked to have a 'reserve pool of unemployed people' to keep wages low. There is little sign of this mechanism having operated in Ireland. The trade unions do not represent unemployed people and have managed to keep pay rates fairly high, especially in the public sector. Workers in the private sector are having to accept some pay cuts on foot of serious job losses. Pay cuts would be far more acceptable if everyone had to 'share the pain equally'. This is not just because of a sense of fairness, but also because of Ireland's strong focus on relativities. It adds insult to injury if the brother-in-law is earning more than we are! It sometimes seems as if a small, homogeneous country is like a family where sibling rivalry is the important dynamic.

It may be that social partnership also drove a wedge between workers and employers. These groups of people do not meet very often on an individual or personal basis. Negotiations were handled by their representatives in a formal setting in Government Buildings. It is not certain what this has done to the relationship between employer and employee, but there is a strong possibility that it has led to a degree of misunderstanding of each side's root concerns. It has always been the case throughout history that a good and decent employer is worth more than trade unions and labour laws put together. Paternalism is not being advocated; rather, employers who understand and feel for the position of workers.

The fact that we have drifted into a clinical, systematic way of sorting out industrial relations suggests that employees may have been too militant and employers too short-sighted to develop good working relationships. It is conceivable that in a small country with no historical class system, it has proved difficult to develop good relationships. Certainly, an Irish worker who has to go cap in hand to his boss to ask for a pay rise would feel demeaned by the experience – and resentful if the request were refused. It is safer to develop structures for this purpose, but that inevitably puts a distance between the parties concerned. Perhaps these distances can be reduced now that social partnership has collapsed.

Another form of bipolarity enters the picture here. It relates to the extraordinary difference between an Irish person in a formal setting and the same person in an informal one-on-one situation. In one setting, the person can be cold and aggressive; in the other, charming and witty. I have no idea why we are so willing and able to don different personae on different occasions. How many times do we hear people say they could hardly recognise their best friend on television? Protean behaviour clearly does not make industrial relations problems any easier.

Nevertheless, Irish employees are probably as good as those in any country, though they do need to be motivated. There is a tendency to spend more time than is warranted chatting in corridors and offices. There tend to be too many meetings and bureaucratic procedures. While this may hurt productivity in the short term, it could have the opposite effect in the longer term owing to networking and team-building. In the knowledge economy, it might even be the case that constructive loafing should be encouraged! The romantic poet John Keats believed that great ideas and inspiration came to those who engaged in 'diligent indolence' – a form of leisure for which 'the craic' is a close analogue.

Irish workers seek more personal freedom than those in other countries. If a boss refuses to allow a worker a day's leave to attend a sporting event or some family occasion, there is a strong possibility that the worker will feign an illness and take the day off anyway. Irish workers tend to have many interests that are not work-related. This may have short-run costs, but it could be argued that outside interests make for more rounded individuals.

Actors and painters often say that it is wonderful to be paid for work they love doing anyway. This really is the key to sustained productivity. If we could match work to cultural preferences, then our economic future would be secure. We can see this revealed preference all around us. For example, it is no coincidence that the public parks in our cities are by and large superbly well maintained. This is because the people who work in those parks enjoy their work and feel fulfilled by it. This may have something to do with our agricultural patrimony. It is precisely this kind of 'coincidence of interests' that is so important to secure the country's economic future. One of the most damaging aspects of colonisation must surely be the repression of the cultural values of the indigenous people. In such circumstances the process of economic growth will not be organic and will be perceived as 'foreign'.

In general, where productivity is less than it should be, it is management that tends to let the side down. It is not clear that managers or executives in Ireland fully realise the importance of decision-making, communicating, and long-term planning. Many are reluctant to give staff more responsibility. A colleague once told me that Irish executives are like football managers who want to take the penalties themselves – because they don't trust the staff to do so. This can be demoralising.

Managers sometimes defend themselves on the grounds that there is always a degree of unpredictability about how staff behave. They may respond well to new challenges, but there is always a risk, however slight, that they will not be cooperative. One manager gave the visit to Ireland of Pope John Paul II as an example. The Office of Public Works staff who arranged the altar and seating in the Phoenix Park worked around the clock and performed miracles, but, according to the lugubrious manager, we do not have the inspiration of St Peter every day.

Mobility

Labour is very mobile in countries like the US where families will move to different states to find work. In Ireland, this kind of mobility is unusual. A person seeking work in Dublin, for example, would be reluctant to cross the Liffey. In the past an unemployed person from Mayo, say, would have found it easier to go to the UK than to Dublin or Cork. It is not clear what gave rise to this attitude. It may be a sense of failure in front of one's peers. In Birmingham or London there is more anonymity and perhaps not as much loss of face, especially since other Irish emigrants would have had similar experiences.

Mobility within Ireland was not a problem for immigrant workers. They did not have strong roots in any particular part of the country. If a builder asked a Polish worker to be on a site in

Cork in the coming week, the Polish worker had no difficulty in going there. Since jobs are now being lost, many foreign workers will look for jobs abroad, but with recession persisting in many other countries as well, it may be difficult to find work. It is not evident, so far at least, that foreign workers are being kept on by Irish firms at the expense of Irish workers.

Lack of mobility has always been a feature of Dublin's inner city, with the result that the unemployment rate there has rarely fallen below 20 per cent. This is probably a good example of 'hysteresis' – the idea that unemployment feeds on itself.[3] Many of the inner-city unemployed come from families where the head of household is also unemployed. There is little expectation of getting a job, and applications for work are rarely even acknowledged because the employer decides that the addresses are on the wrong side of the track. It is no surprise that a relatively high proportion of unemployed youth from the inner cities go into the black market or crime.

Change and the Need for Training

As the economy changes – and we have seen how there is a trend away from manufacturing and towards service industries – the workforce will have to adapt more quickly than ever before. Workers who start out in one sector may find that they have to move to another sector and possibly a third one in their lifetime. This is all part of the process of 'creative destruction', which is one of the fundamental 'laws' of economic development.[4] Horses were replaced by cars and tractors, cruise ships were largely replaced by aeroplanes. To the extent that Ireland moves up the value chain, there will be a growing need for retraining as well as adaptation. The present generation of employees will most likely have to go through three or four major career changes, a notable departure from historical norms.

That is one reason why a good secondary education is important; as well as promising a decent rate of remuneration, it also provides a foundation for further training. In the private sector, where most forms of employment are exposed to the harsh winds of competition, it is essential for staff to be re-trainable. In the sheltered sectors, such as the public service, it is probably not so important from the individual's point of view, though it is essential if the public service is to improve its performance.

In Ireland, the phrase 'well-educated labour force' has become something of a mantra. Unfortunately, the statistics do not fully back up this contention. The proportion of the population aged 25–64 which had completed secondary school education in Ireland in 2005 was 58 per cent, compared with an OECD average of 69 per cent. The proportion in the US was 88 per cent, Sweden 72 per cent, the UK 82 per cent, and France 79 per cent. Forecasts for 2015 showed Ireland in a better position relatively speaking, though still fairly far below the OECD average. There is now evidence of grade inflation, which suggests a significant lowering of educational standards.

Entrepreneurs must also be trained. The bank fiasco in Ireland shows quite clearly that bank executives do not understand the risks involved in many derivative financial products. It also appears that their understanding of basic economics in relation to the property market is woefully inadequate. Most banking done in Ireland is of the simple 'plain vanilla' variety, so it is extremely difficult to understand how such egregious mistakes were made. Clearly, the standard of entrepreneurship was very low.

If we are serious about becoming an information economy, it is essential that we train the trainers; for example, making sure that science teachers in particular are fully up to date with their own discipline and with more advanced teaching techniques.

Third-level degrees do go out of date. Some years ago it was estimated that the 'melting degree' of a primary qualification in
engineering was twelve; that is, after twelve years the degree was
effectively worthless unless the engineer in question had made
strenuous efforts to update himself. It is bizarre that highly
qualified post-doctoral researchers in Ireland are paid less than
gardaí, prison officers and tradesmen. These pay relativities are
reversed in the US which is truly an information economy.

With regard to innovation and technology, one of the most
encouraging developments took place in early March 2009. Two
universities, UCD and TCD, decided to combine forces for their
scientific research. The initiative put a morsel of flesh on an earlier rather skeletal report by government on the smart economy.[5] No sooner had the presidents of both universities announced their joint initiative, however, than the presidents of
the other five universities complained that they were being shut
out. One president referred to the possibility of civil war between the universities. Here again, the ubiquitous 'split' rears its
ugly head. Even if the universities – and institutes of technology
– do manage to cooperate with each other, and even if important research is done, there is still the question of entrepreneurship and the challenge of converting research into commercial
possibilities. In short, there are many awkward bridges to be
crossed in Ireland before reaching the stage where employees
can put new technologies to practical use.

The much-vaunted capitalist system is likely to be seriously
questioned in the aftermath of the international banking disaster
of 2008. Nevertheless, it is likely that privatisation will continue,
though at a slower pace. This is a form of discontinuous change
which can unsettle employees. People who work for a public sector body usually fear such change and they and their trade unions
tend to mount strong opposition. The privatisation of Aer Lingus

clearly caused distress and conflict which show no signs of abating. Workers find it very difficult to change from a culture of secure employment to one of exposure to competition and the ever-present threat of job losses. They continue to believe that the strike weapon will work, whereas it might only push the company towards bankruptcy. There is no bail-out on offer for private-sector companies (except banks!). Nevertheless, it is the job of management to 'sell' the new culture to the staff. Fear of uncertainty is often paralysing to employees.

I recall a situation where a staff member deservedly won promotion but had to transfer to another section. She was most reluctant to change, although it meant going just fifty metres down the corridor! She was prepared to forego the promotion to stay in her comfort zone. After applying as much pressure as I could, she agreed to move. In less than two weeks she told me that she loved her new job. This was entirely predictable but, because of an initial fear of the unknown, she had been prepared to jeopardise her career.

Managing the Workforce

As a general proposition, Irish workers are probably a little more sensitive than their counterparts in Europe and North America. They will react badly to criticism, especially from an Irish boss. Because there is no class system as such, the boss cannot appear too high-handed without being dubbed a 'poser'. We do not like hierarchies and, in recent years, have come to question the hierarchical structure of the church. One often hears remarks like, 'Who does he think he is?' 'I remember him at school; he was no Einstein.' In most cases, the person who has been criticised by a boss takes it much too personally. I am aware of staff appraisal sessions that ended in fisticuffs! No doubt ancestral voices contribute to hurt feelings and wounded pride. These unsettling

voices come not only from our colonial past but also from oppression and abuse by the institutional church, directed against
young, vulnerable people.

Managers should recognise the culture of their workforce.
There are different ways of offering criticism and the best way is
to emphasise the person's strong points at the same time as
pointing out shortcomings. It is surprising that this is so rare
because Irish people are still fairly homogeneous as a cultural
group and we should be well able to put ourselves in the other
person's shoes. In management-speak, this is called 'inter-
subjectivity', and Irish bosses ought to practice it a lot more than
they do. Unfortunately, they tend to be circumlocutory rather
than 'straight from the shoulder'. This doesn't help anyone.

The best boss I ever had always asked me for my opinion. He
would ruminate about what he thought should be done and
then he would follow up with, 'What do *you* think?' Such a simple question, but what a difference it made, what an effect on
morale! That individual had no management training whatsoever and had no time for it, but he was a 'born' manager.

There have been some high-profile instances of poor interpersonal behaviour. The most famous one, which divided the
country, was the expulsion of Roy Keane from Saipan in the 2002
World Cup. Was he right or was the manager, Mick McCarthy,
right? Another case related to the Beijing Olympics in 2008
where a swimmer's goggles fell off during a race because the
team had brought the wrong swim hats! Other instances include
the extraordinarily poor showing of the Irish team at the Rugby
World Cup in 2007 where there were management/player problems in the camp, and problems in Cork hurling where the top
players refused to cooperate with the appointed manager (who
eventually resigned). Such incidents are frequent, and they do
not seem to happen in other countries to anything like the same

extent. It is important to stress, however, that the difficulties are rarely the fault of the sportsmen or women, but rather of the organisers. This adds support to the view that management is usually at fault.

A debacle involving Ryanair and the then Tánaiste in February 2010 serves as an example of management failure in the business area. Ryanair's Chief Executive, Michael O'Leary, said that he could provide 500 well paid jobs in aircraft maintenance in a hangar recently vacated by SR Technics. The Tánaiste did not want to talk to him. Aer Lingus and the Dublin Airport Authority did not wish to cooperate in the venture. The jobs were lost. There is something wrong about how we manage our affairs. Small problems are blown out of proportion, people take offence, hidden agendas are imputed, there is an inability to compromise, and a high degree of stubbornness. Eccentric behaviour is usually interpreted as aggressive and wrong-headed, whereas it is most often based on anxiety and insecurity.

An interesting hypothesis is that Irish employees work harder for foreign bosses; for example, in American companies based here. Unfortunately, there is no data to test this, but there is some evidence to suggest that Irish employees raise their game when they go abroad. Indeed, they frequently become highly successful in other countries.

Profit-sharing has never been seriously tried in Ireland. Employers say that workers wouldn't take a cut in pay in hard times. Employees claim that true profitability would not be revealed by management. The unions are generally opposed to forms of profit-sharing, probably on the grounds that such schemes might undermine their influence. Yet, for people who like to be consulted and to debate issues, some form of profit-sharing could work very well.

The Future for Jobs

It is possible that in the future the labour force will split into
three broad groups. The first group will be the manager/owner
group whose specialty will be judgment. This is one of the few
skills that cannot be replicated by computers. It is likely that, in
addition to technical knowledge, members of this group will
have a rounded education which should enable them to make
sound decisions on the basis of complex yet incomplete data. As
economies become more globalised and interconnected, it is
likely that the demand for 'renaissance' men and women will
increase.

The second group of workers will be the super-tekkies and
innovators – the people who invent the machines, the software
and the systems. These workers will probably be paid more or
less on a par with the renaissance managers. Intellectual property rights, such as patents and copyrights, will be very important to keep this group motivated. The balance of power may
shift in favour of this group because they will tend to be head-
hunted. At the lower end of this group will be those who know
how to maintain and operate the machines and systems.

The third group will include those who have little technical
expertise. This will be a low-paid group, and probably a diminishing one over time. It will be difficult for these workers to be
upwardly mobile, and governments may have to put considerable resources into up-skilling. There will be a diminishing demand for this kind of labour, except in some specific fields such
as health care, particularly for the elderly.

As far as education is concerned, the emphasis on science
will continue to increase. It is likely that medicine, teaching and
even law will become more and more computerised so that ex-
ponents in these professions will also be expected to have a

grounding in scientific subjects. Bank executives will have to understand the mathematics of complex derivative products, especially after the weaknesses exposed in the financial collapses of 2008.

As smart economies develop, it is likely that the demand for the first two groups will grow quickly. Many people might not be able to qualify for these groups and might find it hard to get reasonably paid jobs. It is possible that unemployment rates will trend upwards. Smart economies, however, will tend to be highly productive so that, with reasonably good government, social welfare benefits should be able to take care of those who fall behind in the science race.

To get science subjects more deeply embedded in the secondary school curriculum, it seems desirable to allow more points for mathematics, physics and related subjects than for other courses. Science teachers should be incentivised by higher pay, in return for which they should accept more frequent inspections and performance assessments.

Employment in a Recession

In the present recession, jobs are being lost every day and employees are on tenterhooks. The government, prompted by the EU, has adopted a deflationary policy that could do long-term damage to confidence which had been hard won in the good years. Employees are being asked to make sacrifices. Most resistance is coming from public-sector unions, who argue that the burden is not being shared equally. This is true in the sense that there is a group of über-rich who can shelter their income in many different ways, including schemes set up by the government. It is not clear, however, that equity can be fully achieved. There remains a suspicion that shock and uncertainty are weighing more heavily on people than a desire for equity. Moreover, pay cuts affect people's perceptions of themselves; this kind of sensitivity may or may not derive from the Brehon Laws which embraced the notion of 'honour-price' or a person's rank in society. Uncertainty is an additional factor because there is no overall plan and no one knows how deep the recession will go or how long it will last.

To save costs, employers are letting staff go, but it would be much better if staff could be consulted in advance about part-time working or ways to improve productivity. The costs to employers of losing skilled people can be greater than they realise. These costs might relate to the image of the company concerned, the possibility that highly talented people may join a competitor firm, the poor effect on morale of those remaining, and the costs of re-hiring later on.[6] The costs to the government (and taxpayer) of growing unemployment are also very high.

In this climate of uncertainty, it may be argued that employees in the private sector will work even harder in an attempt to save their jobs, but this might not be true in the public sector where there is virtual job security. The pension levy on public officials, combined with pay cuts, may have a demoralising effect. To make matters worse, the pay cuts which were applied to the most senior civil servants were subsequently rescinded. The majority of less well paid public servants see this as an affront. Not only is there a conflict between the public and private sectors, but there is also a split within the public sector itself.

Concluding Comments

Employees are important to the growth of the economy. To maximise their contribution to growth, they need to be efficient, mobile, flexible, and capable of being retrained. Irish employees are probably as competent and productive as any in the world, but they tend to have a low boredom threshold and to take offence too easily. On occasion they might appear to be angular or uncooperative, but this usually masks feelings of insecurity. Indifferent management is often the root cause of poor employee morale.

The vocational element that used to be present in many of the professions, especially the 'caring' ones, seems to be much less in evidence nowadays. That is not to say, though, that workers will use their skills only in exchange for money. There are still many examples of philanthropic work being performed in every walk of life. This is because we follow social norms as well as market norms.[7]

Productivity would be improved by greater diligence and attention to detail. However, the greatest scope for productivity improvements resides in the use of new technologies. This may involve re-training and a degree of flexibility on the part of employees. The training arms of the state must be reformed as a matter of urgency.

It would help enormously if managers consulted their employees more frequently and involved them more in the decision-making process. To some extent, our employer/labour structures tend to obviate the need for close interaction between managers and employees at the level of the individual firm. The Labour Relations Commission stated in July 2010 that it was 'overwhelmed' by the number of industrial relations disputes with which it has to deal. One wonders how many of these issues could, and should, have been resolved by the management and workers involved.

Although high and growing unemployment is the priority problem, resentment and poor morale, resulting from pay cuts and pension levies, are likely to inhibit productivity among those who are still employed. Further industrial relations problems and demonstrations seem likely.

8

IRELAND'S GROWTH PROSPECTS

'It's a great little country ... a pity we make such a hames of it.' – Overheard in a pub

This chapter will briefly try to bring together the culture-induced behaviours of the important economic groupings discussed earlier, that is, entrepreneurs, public servants and politicians, consumers and employees. Such behaviours will largely determine our ability to cope with recession and our economic future over the next decade and beyond.

A focus on culture-induced behaviours is not meant to downplay exogenous factors such as discoveries of natural resources, changes in oil prices, exchange rates, foreign direct investment and so on. It simply recognises the fact that in the long term it is we ourselves who will shape our economic destiny. In fact, our economic future will be more of our own making than in previous decades because all the external factors that helped us in the past will be far less influential, such as foreign direct investment, EU subsidies to agriculture, structural and cohesion funds, reliance on foreign borrowing by government, currency depreciation, and the sharp fall in interest rates caused by EMU membership. Having to persevere without most or all these external benefits will not be easy. No doubt FDI will pick up in due course but we should regard that as a bonus and not as an innate part of the economy. We must stop taking credit for the high performance of US multinationals based here.

It is better to be realistic rather than aspirational. We are not, for example, going to become 'the innovation island' or the Silicon Valley of Europe just because the government aspires to that goal.[1] The fact that a relatively high proportion of young Irish people would like to become entrepreneurs is not very convincing – the proportion is actually higher in Greece. The important question remains: Do we as a people have the will and the ability to secure a good economic future for ourselves and the next generation?

The Enterprise Deficit

It was suggested in earlier chapters that our long-term policy of depending on foreign direct investment may have weakened the development of domestic entrepreneurship. We were able to achieve vigorous economic growth without too much effort on our part. Ireland is a dual economy, with high productivity in the 'foreign' or modern sector, and low productivity in the domestic or indigenous sector. This dual structure has been obvious for decades but, surprisingly, it has never influenced official thinking or policy-making to any noticeable degree. It has been taken for granted, and no alternative industrial strategy was formulated in the last fifty years, even on a contingency basis.

Because of our loss of competitiveness, the opening up of China, EU pressure for tax harmonisation, and a possible change in US tax legislation and industrial policy, we will have to depend much more on home-grown enterprise in the future. There is another reason for this. Most of the important US multinational firms already have a presence in Ireland; it is possible that this may set some sort of natural upper limit to further invest-ment from that source.

Unfortunately, despite a few notable success stories, it does not seem as if domestic entrepreneurial skills in Ireland are suf-ficiently widespread to develop the supply-side of the economy very rapidly over the coming decades. There is ample evidence of high skill levels in the arts, and in many other fields, but en-trepreneurship is another matter, especially where the develop-ment and long-term sustainability of innovative businesses are concerned. Indeed, our financial and property-related entrepre-neurship is poorly regarded at home and abroad.

Without radical decisions there will be no innovation. This is clearly problematic in the development of a 'smart' economy, which is now essential since we have lost competitiveness in more traditional forms of manufacturing. A study undertaken in 2007 found Ireland to be very far down the innovation scale,[2] despite all the official rhetoric to the contrary. Still, this does not mean that good research is not being undertaken; it is more a question of how to develop the fruits of research in a sound commercial manner. In many cases, the results of impressive research are sold to foreign companies rather than developed here.

It is not clear how we are supposed to transform ourselves into a smart economy. We have excellent scientists and an im-pressive tradition in science – as the names of Boyle, Boole, Hamilton and Walton testify – but scientists often have little in-terest in the commercial side of things. And entrepreneurs are not particularly interested in science. The hyphenated scientist-entrepreneur is a very rare breed in Ireland. How to square this circle is not immediately apparent.

The IDA has placed advertisements in *Time* magazine and *The Economist* – ads that over-egg the pudding. For example:

The Irish. Creative. Imaginative. And flexible. Agile minds with a unique capacity to initiate, and innovate, without being directed. Always thinking on their feet ... generating new knowledge and new ideas.... This flexible attitude pervades the ecosystem.... With its innate knowledge and flexibility, the Irish mind can be the pathway to profit for your business.

The extraordinary thing about these ads is not just the hyperbole, but the fact that if we have all these talents why are we advertising for foreign multinationals in the first place? Maybe we do have great ideas but are unable to commercialise them without an injection of foreign entrepreneurship.

The IDA and the Minister for Enterprise, Trade and Innovation, Batt O'Keefe, argued in June 2010, on the basis of some psychometric testing, that Irish executives were more likely than their counterparts to engage in 'right-brain thinking', and consequently have intuitive and imaginative skills required for entrepreneurship. The Minister believes that 'we Irish think and act in a unique and agile way'. This may all be true, but it is difficult to see how these talents, essential in the arts, equip us for the rough and tumble of the marketplace.

The enterprise deficit could be serious because there is not much the government can do in a small, open economy which does not have its own interest rate or exchange rate. If foreign direct investment continues to be affected by the US recession, tax harmonisation and by our loss of competitiveness, then it is unlikely that Irish entrepreneurs will emerge in sufficient numbers. The ability to take risks is not greatly in evidence, and is often undermined by the 'tall poppy syndrome'.

There is no Irish equivalent of Nokia and it is difficult to see such a company emerging here. We do of course have impres-

sive multinational companies like Glanbia and Cement Road-
stone Holdings, but these tend to be medium-to-low technology
companies and not fully consistent with the government's aspi-
ration to transform Ireland into a 'smart' economy.

The Leadership Deficit

Not surprisingly, politicians and public servants do not display
many entrepreneurial traits. Politicians are often elected on the
basis of family dynasties and tend to be too focused on short-
term and local issues. The tradition of cronyism is, unfortunately, alive and well in Ireland. No political party of any hue
has ever seriously questioned the system of political appointments that has bedevilled the country for fifty years – appointments that are routinely made (on a tribal or clan basis) without
any reference to ability, qualifications or suitability. Mediocrity
is embedded in our system of governance. Far too few political
appointees – or ministers for that matter – have any business
experience.

As we've seen, politicians are slow to make decisions and are
always seeking outcomes where there are no losers. These are
extremely rare; in most cases some people have to lose in order
to achieve the greater good. It is the losers who will cry foul and
threaten not to vote for the politician(s) in question. For this
reason, politicians often avoid decisions which could serve the
common good.

In his television series *The Limits of Liberty*, Diarmaid Fer-
riter argued that many of the founders of the state believed in a
controlling elite (which was completely at odds with the concept
of a republic), favoured emigration by the less able, and set the
scene for the mistreatment of children. To the extent that this is
true, it may well explain the present bail-out of bankers at the
expense of ordinary people. At a more mundane level, however,

recent governments have been inefficient and uncaring. Increasingly, deficiencies in decision-making and in assuming responsibility are covered up by spin doctors and PR gurus. Hype has almost completely replaced substance. Or, as Declan Kiberd puts it, 'gesture has triumphed over structure'.

For years the Ahern/Cowen government was at pains to criticise commentators who expressed concern about the Irish economy. Then, when the recession struck and the government had to look for pay cuts, it reversed engines and started to 'talk down' the economy in an effort to soften up the unions. Politicians spoke of the most serious recession in 100 years – all caused by external factors! The result was that the government destroyed any shred of confidence that remained. It also undermined its own credibility and leadership role.

Corruption has led to poor urban planning decisions and the misallocation of resources. It is difficult to prove fraud or corruption in this country, partly because it is difficult to prove an *intention* to defraud, and it is most unlikely that the tribunals of inquiry will clean out the Augean stables. There are many surreptitious forms of fraud that leave no paper trail or evidence of any sort. What is to stop a political figure from phoning a business friend to let him know the lowest bid for a government contract, thus giving him the opportunity of winning it? Cash can change hands without leaving any fingerprints. We can only hope that people in power will behave properly; it is difficult to legislate for morality. Apart from the active encouragement of whistle-blowing, it is hard to see how good behaviour can be assured. However, our cultural 'take' on whistle-blowing is ambivalent, to say the least. For many people, it is equivalent to informing.

Bad behaviour destroys the credibility needed for leadership. We have seen this happen in the church as well as in politics; few people believe in these institutions any more. In economic life, trust is a vital ingredient which enables thousands of trans-actions to take place every day. We have recently seen what happens to banks when they lose the trust of their depositors. The effects on the economy can be equally devastating.

Despite many promises of reform, and many studies, there has been no action. The much-vaunted strategic management initiative did not deliver the goods. Now that the government is trying to cope with a severe recession and a banking crisis, there is little prospect of proportionate public sector reform. Fire-fighting has taken over from strategic thinking. In a climate of pay cuts the hope of radical reform is a vain one. The Croke Park deal is likely to be accepted, but it is doubtful if the government will really grasp the nettle of public sector reform.

This is tragic because it is possible that such reform could save the national exchequer up to €4-5 billion per annum. Ire-land could largely solve its fiscal problems, and avoid the danger of being too identified with Greece. The government, however, prefers to target taxpayers, presumably because they are a large amorphous group with little lobbying power.

There is no overall economic plan. The framework document on the smart economy was roundly criticised. The Minister for Finance said that the criticism was unfair because the document in question was not a plan. Two days later the Tánaiste referred to it as a 'comprehensive plan'. This causes uncertainty and is not consistent with the kind of leadership which is so badly needed.

The Prospects for Consumers

Consumer spending is an important component of economic growth, especially in the short run. The question is whether or not consumers have the disposable income, confidence and other incentives to go to the shops and spend money. Irish con-sumers tend to be motivated by much the same factors as in other countries. In other words, there are fewer peculiarly Irish quirks at play when it comes to consumption. However, there are some.

Despite some notable exceptions, Irish people as a whole did not define themselves by the quantity and quality of the goods and services they managed to acquire in the good years. For the most part, they did not subscribe to the philosophy, 'I shop, therefore I am'. People still judged each other by who they were rather than by what they had.

The fact that the population is ageing, albeit more slowly than in other developed countries, may also restrain consumer spending. An American comedian, Jackie Mason, once observed, 'I have enough money to last me the rest of my life, as long as I don't buy anything'. In early 2010 the government brought in proposals for pension provision in the future. Employers and employees are going to be forced to make greater contributions; this will be another factor weighing on current consumption.

If prices in general were to fall, consumers might be encouraged to spend more than they otherwise would. We have seen many Irish consumers travelling to Northern Ireland and even to North America to shop because of lower prices there. Appealing to national loyalty is unlikely to succeed where budgets are tight and people have households to run. Nor should it be otherwise in a global economy.

Irish retailers have traditionally been reluctant to lower their prices because of market conditions, but in the present recession there is, thankfully, some evidence of price flexibility, at least in Dublin. This should be of some help, although the consumer's response to lower prices will be less than hoped for owing to lower disposable income and the threat of job losses. Some retailers are being less than honest, however. Consumers are being lured into shops by promises of price reductions that are exaggerated. Estate agents have argued that property prices have bottomed out, even though a UCD study shows that there is still excess supply of some 300,000 dwelling units. Dishonest claims are counter-productive.

Falling prices can be a double-edged sword, however, as we know from the generalised deflation in Japan in the 1990s. If consumers believe that prices are going to continue to fall, they might withhold consumption now in the hope of lower prices later on. While Irish consumers tend not to look too far ahead, this still poses a risk, especially in a period of severe recession with tight fiscal and monetary policy.

Between 1995 and 2008, consumers were often accused of being materialistic and of losing their moral compass. This was nonsense and it is to be hoped that it will have no effect on consumer decisions now or in the future. The last thing we need is another guilt complex.

The Prospects for Employees

Now that jobs are being lost, many people are discovering how upsetting this is, and would probably opt for re-employment, even at lower wages. For those in the public sector who have secure employment and good pay and pension provision, there is a strong reluctance to accept lower wages or even a pension levy.

Social partnership has to some extent driven a wedge between personal productivity and remuneration. In other words, since many wages are negotiated centrally, the individual worker has little sense of the kind of performance expected of them. Poor communications in the office or on the factory floor can undermine commitment. The management of people as a means of production often comes across as manipulative and condescending.

Pay and career prospects are very attractive in law, medicine, business studies, banking, and less so for science and engineering.

There will undoubtedly be jobs in business and financial services for lawyers, tax experts and accountants, but in general this does not augur well for the development of a 'smart' economy. The attractions for scientists are much greater in the US and there will continue to be a brain drain. Even if Ireland does succeed in moving up the value chain, it is more than likely that we will lose many more industrial jobs than we can create high value-added ones. For example, we are likely to lose more jobs in precision-tool manufacturing than we will be able to create in genetic research. This will also further skew income distribution.

Employees can hardly be expected to get the economy going again; this is a job for entrepreneurs and, to some extent, for government. Employees cannot take major initiatives at the macro level, yet they are asked to make sacrifices so as to lower costs and restore competitiveness. This has led to a fraught situation and there may well be strikes. It is a pity that employees in general have not, over the years, been given a sense of their true importance and consulted more about issues that affect their own workplaces. Employees and their unions tend to reject wage moderation and improved work practices, partly because of standard-of-living considerations, but also because of pride and a desire to prevent their already low position in the hierarchy from sinking further. This is especially true when other groups, such as bankers, lawyers and politicians, are not called on to make equivalent adjustments. The 'memory of inherited dissent' – to use Gus Martin's phrase – is never far below the surface.

Looking Ahead

Despite Ireland's many remarkable achievements in literature, music, theatre and sports, it seems that we do not have any special talent for developing the economy. An imaginative people might regard this as a mundane activity, and it probably explains why our best economic performances have been dominated by foreign direct investment. If flows of FDI resume on the scale observed during the Celtic Tiger period, there will not be much to worry about; but if this does not happen, there is cause to be concerned about the indigenous economy.

It will take some time to recover from the present recession and we are unlikely to meet the fiscal target set by the government (and Brussels) of reducing the general government deficit to 3 per cent of GDP, even though the target year has been extended from 2013 to 2014. There is a possibility that the recession could last significantly beyond 2011, especially if civil unrest frightens off potential investors. Clearly our attitudes and behaviour will play a part in the recovery from recession and will also dictate how the economy will perform in the longer term.

The Celtic Tiger period from 1995 to 2001 witnessed a growth rate of about 9 per cent per annum, and between 2001 and 2007 the growth rate slowed to some 4.5 per cent, but was still very respectable by international standards. The first period was largely driven by foreign direct investment from the US and the second period by consumer spending and construction-related activity, both of which were unsustainable in the longer term, especially since they depended to a considerable extent on borrowing from banks.

Real GNP fell by 3 per cent in 2008 and by 8 per cent in 2009. Although the ESRI and Department of Finance expect some positive growth in 2010 and 2011, this may be a little optimistic. Even if there is some modest growth, it will be mainly because of pharmaceutical exports, the profits of which will be repatriated to the US. Consequently, Irish living standards may not rise. It also seems likely that the unemployment rate could reach 14 per cent before the recession runs its course, unless the historical safety-valve of emigration comes into play.

There is no denying that our fiscal situation is precarious or that the government has to reduce the deficit which has been bloated by the bail-out of Anglo Irish Bank. Failure to act would result in higher borrowing costs being levied by international markets. The government has not admitted that its present approach to fiscal adjustment is deflationary. One wonders if some other means could have been found to manage the deficit while at the same time lessening the deflationary effects. Inadequate consideration has been given to less conventional measures such as:

- Saving €4-5 billion a year for at least two years by genuine public sector reform, eliminating fraud and inefficiency.

- Selling state assets and outsourcing state services; this seems to have been put on the agenda at last.

- Substituting domestic borrowing for external borrowing. If the terms of the national recovery bonds and indeed Post Office savings were made more attractive, the service and repayment of such debt would go back into the Irish economy rather than going abroad. (It is ironic that if the government had not provided guarantees for Anglo Irish Bank and Irish Nationwide, a large proportion of their deposits would have been transferred to the Post Office, that is, into the government's own coffers.)

- Borrowing from other governments rather than the markets. Goodwill between governments can sometimes result in better terms and conditions than those imposed by the markets.

- Stopping the practice of putting about €1.5 billion per annum into the National Pension Reserve Fund. It is unlikely that the rate of return on the money would ever equal the high rate at which it is borrowed.

- Introducing property taxation that would include all property, including land and commercial buildings.

- Reintroducing third-level education fees but with a cheaper and more equitable student loan scheme with means-testing.

- Prioritising government spending in a way that favours job creation.

The key point is to ensure that fiscal adjustment does not prolong the recession or lead to a situation where unemployment becomes entrenched. At the time of writing, September 2010, the government seems to be leaning towards expenditure cuts rather than tax increases for the 2011 budget. But there has been little discussion of the less conventional approaches mentioned above. There is every reason to expect another deflationary budget in 2011 – adjustment fatigue may not fully set in until the following year as the next general election approaches.

After the recession, we should be able to get on a long-term growth path of some 2 per cent per annum. The immediate recovery years could be slightly above that rate. A dead cat will bounce if it falls far enough. But the growth rate is likely to settle down to 2 per cent, or thereabouts, over the longer term, say fifteen to twenty years. If foreign direct investment resumes, it should be regarded as a bonus. We can hope for the best as long as we prepare for the worst.

In trying to peer into the future, it is useful to distinguish between a short-term recovery from recession and the longer-term future, up to about 2030. Some of our short-term indicators – retail sales, VAT receipts, order books, manufacturing output and competitiveness – are beginning to stabilise but others are not. The signals are mixed.

The most depressing indicator relates to unemployment. We have seen how the numbers on the Live Register rose to 453,000 in June 2010. This truly frightening figure had increased by over 37,000 since the previous June and would have been higher if not for net emigration during the year. In the following July the numbers on the Live Register rose to 467,000 – a big increase even when seasonally adjusted. There is a serious risk that many unskilled people will be left jobless, especially in younger age groups. As was noted earlier, this kind of unemployment has an unfortunate tendency to become entrenched, partly because of the 'discouraged worker syndrome'. There have been years when real GNP grew quite robustly without any perceptible fall in the numbers out of work. This gave rise to the terms 'jobless growth' and 'the statistical economy'.

We may be facing a broadly similar situation at the present time. The ESRI believes that some 40,000 workers will be laid off in the public sector over the next four years as the government tries to achieve another €8 billion in exchequer savings. The ESRI admits that fiscal rectitude will be deflationary, slowing down the economy by about 1 per cent per year (something the government tends not to mention). We also know that AIB and Bank of Ireland plan to reduce staff numbers by about 2,000, while other companies, such as Eircom, are talking about substantial redundancies. It seems that many companies look to lay-offs as a means of restoring competitiveness. Apart from the social costs of continuing unemployment, this means it is going to be more difficult for the government to achieve its fiscal targets.

Another negative indicator is the continuing uncertainty about whether or not the US has turned the corner. Some commentators believe there could be a 'soft spot' or even another recession in the US fairly soon, possibly when the positive effects of President Obama's stimulus package run out. If the American economy remains sluggish then so will world trade and direct investment overseas.

Finally, while the international markets often exaggerate matters, they usually get the general direction right. Up to September 2010, they were still looking askance at Ireland Inc. This may be construed as another negative sign.

So while many Irish commentators believe that recovery is around the corner, this seems optimistic. It is not being suggested that there will be a second 'dip' – let us hope not – but there is no guarantee that when the economy hits bottom it will suddenly bounce back. It could stay on the bottom for a longer period than many expect. In other words, the recession could prove to be U-shaped rather than V-shaped. Indeed, one could not rule out a Japanese-style L.

The government has not inspired confidence. The significant fiscal adjustments of 2009 and 2010 were partly driven by the guidelines of the EU, without regard to possible deflationary consequences on the Irish economy. Because of the latter, plus social unrest and the possible collapse of the Fianna Fáil party, it is by no means clear that this kind of adjustment can be continued over the following two years. International evidence suggests that 'adjustment fatigue' sets in after about two years. The Croke Park agreement may well be the first sign of fatigue on the government's side.

Wages are too high to allow us to compete well internationally. Utility costs are also high and, despite the fall in property prices, the rents of many commercial properties are legally obliged to go up instead of down! Various bank bail-outs – deposit guarantees, recapitalisation, nationalisation and the creation of a 'bad bank' (NAMA), which was approved by the EU in February 2010 – have not yet resulted in renewed lending for businesses. To make matters worse, banks began to increase their lending interest rates in early 2010 in order to restore profitability. This action is the equivalent of tighter monetary policy, which is the last thing the economy needs in a recession. Over 60 per cent of small and medium-sized industries are being refused credit; and the other 40 per cent are going to have to pay more for it to compensate for the past mistakes of the banks. Ireland is now in the bizarre situation where, in the middle of a major recession, the two main instruments of policy – fiscal and monetary – have been tightened!

Despite Ireland's compliance with EU fiscal guidelines, the international financial markets do not seem to be very impressed and are inclined to bracket us together with Greece, although the risk premia on Irish government bonds are lower than those on Greek bonds. Ireland is also getting a bad reputation as a tax haven and an offshore location with lax regulation. To the extent that this is true – and it is by no means clear that countries such as Switzerland, Luxembourg and Dubai are more virtuous in this regard – we can see the culture of stroke-play and crony capitalism at work. It could be argued that the Eurozone has already bailed out Ireland in an IMF-style adjustment programme. The European Central Bank has been a major source of liquidity for Irish banks and this role will be increased dramatically under NAMA. The ECB has also bought Irish government debt under its policy of quantitative easing. It is possible that these support arrangements could be made more formal in the coming months. A rescue package has been announced for Greece and there is ongoing discussion about the creation of a European Monetary Fund. The corollary of such measures will be a much closer scrutiny of national budgets and a consequent loss of sovereignty. It is rumoured that Ireland's preferential corporate tax rate could be threatened. There is probably only a grain of truth in this but the fact that such alarming discussions are taking place, gives an indication of the prevailing pessimism. It would be preferable if Ireland could sort out its own problems without any additional conditions being imposed by the Eurozone countries.

How might we cope when the worst of the recession blows over? The wild card is foreign direct investment. If that recovers, there will not be a great deal to worry about, although the duality and bipolarity of the economy will continue. But if FDI does not recover, then we will have to rely almost exclusively on the indigenous economy. What kind of growth path can we expect in that event?

Before the recession, most economists believed that the long-term sustainable growth of the Irish economy, including the foreign sector, was about 4.5 per cent per annum, or possibly even higher. This placed us well ahead of the US where the equivalent figure is about 2.5 per cent, and well above the EU, which comes in at less than 2 per cent. There was, however, an implicit assumption that FDI would continue to be as strong a driver of growth in Ireland as it was in the boom years.

One of the reasons the US had better long-term prospects than the EU was because of the free enterprise nature of that economy, as opposed to the more interventionist and inflexible Europe which never really found a cure for Eurosclerosis even after the Lisbon Agenda.[3] It is not yet clear how the banking fiasco and recession on both sides of the Atlantic might affect long-term growth rates. It is likely, however, that they will be revised down slightly unless there is some major new technological breakthrough. The bloated financial sectors of the large economies will tend to shrink over the next decade or so, and this may have a downward effect on overall growth, although there could be a tendency for resources released from financial sectors to be used in more productive activities, such as pharmaceuticals or information technology.

For the indigenous Irish economy, it is hard to envisage a long-term growth rate significantly above 2 per cent per annum. It is one thing to have caught up on GNP per head in the developed world, but to continue to grow faster would be hard to justify even in the most favourable circumstances. Indeed, a 2 per cent long-term growth path for the indigenous economy is probably optimistic in that it assumes that wage restraint and productivity improvements in the three years from 2009 to 2011 will have restored Ireland's competitiveness. But if there are similar trends in other countries, or if the exchange rate of the euro increases, we may not be able to restore our competitiveness. The 2 per cent growth scenario also assumes that during the same period the problems with our banks will have been sorted out and that 'normal' lending will have resumed – possibly on the basis of nationalisation or foreign takeovers. Both assumptions are optimistic.

Table 5 sets out how a base-line growth rate of about 2 per cent per annum might be broken down across the main national accounts components.

Table 5: Contributions to Base-Line Growth (Indigenous)

Expenditure	(%)	Income	(%)	Output	(%)
Consumption	2.25	Wages	1.75	Manufacturing	1.75
Investment	3.5	Profits	2.5	Construction	2
Government	2			Agriculture	1
Exports	2			Services	2.75
–Imports	2.5				
GNP =	2	GNP =	2	GNP =	2

When economists talk about 'growth rates' they mean the growth in GNP (or GDP). As can be seen from Table 5, GNP measures the total output in a given year. It also shows how this generates income (wages and profit) and allows us to consume, import, invest and buy government services. Clearly, if real GNP grows fast our standards of living will also improve quickly.

It can be seen that investment would have to grow at about 3.5 per cent per annum to support overall growth of 2 per cent. For investment to grow at this rate, profits would have to be relatively buoyant, say about 2.5 per cent per annum.

Imports are expected to increase more quickly than exports over the medium term. Depending on the terms of trade, this could imply a chronic balance-of-payments deficit. The contribution of net exports could, of course, be much greater if foreign direct investment were to pick up. But this should be regarded as a bonus and not something built into the base-line projection, which is purely an indigenous one. It is unlikely that we will fully regain cost competitiveness any time soon.

Wage growth of about 1.75 per cent seems to be consistent with consumption growth of 2.25 per cent, though this might imply some reduction in household savings ratios over time.

On the output side, it is hard to see agriculture growing by more than 1 per cent per annum, or construction and manufacturing by more than 2 per cent. During the recession many small and medium-sized manufacturing and retail companies went to the wall, partly because of the credit crunch. It will take years to re-build the productive capacity. In line with international trends, the services sector is likely to grow by about 2.75 per cent. This will happen only if there is a strong focus on innovative services which can be marketed abroad. If there is a marked reduction in financial sectors abroad, following the present crisis, this forecast could be too optimistic.

There will be years when the economy will grow by more than 2 per cent per annum and years when it will grow by less, but there will be a tendency to 'mean-revert' to an average of 2 per cent. This kind of performance will not be enough to provide full employment and we will probably have to tolerate an unemployment rate of some 10–12 per cent over the long-run, though it could be less if net emigration increases. We will probably never again be in a situation where we have to encourage immigrants into the country to keep the economy booming.

The high rate of unemployment should keep the rate of wage increases fairly modest on average, at least in the exposed sectors of the economy. To the extent that we do become a 'smart' economy, those who work in the high-tech service and IT fields will earn relatively good wages, reflecting their high skills. In general, there will be a much closer relationship between wages and productivity. This will mean changes in pay relativities. Employees (including teachers) with third- and fourth-level qualifications in science subjects and engineering will earn more than bankers, doctors and lawyers.

If an indigenous smart economy does not materialise, then a 2 per cent rate of growth might be optimistic, bearing in mind the thousands of traditional manufacturing jobs that are going to be lost to less developed countries, where wage rates are less than one-fifth of Ireland's.

The growth-convergence literature[4] suggests that a country starting from a lower economic base will tend to catch up on its peers. Hence it will have a faster rate of growth during the catch-up period. This is one of the explanations of the Celtic Tiger phenomenon. But, having caught up – which we did – there is no reason to believe that we would continue to grow faster. It is much more likely that the 'converged' country would merely grow in the future at the same rate as its peers. This is partly because the initial advantages of lower costs have disappeared, which is exactly what happened in Ireland.

As the growth rate settles down to about 2 per cent, and continues at around that rate for the next fifteen years or so, the incentive to invest will be much weaker. During the Celtic Tiger years we had an abnormal situation where the growth rate greatly exceeded the real interest rate. For most of the period, growth was an astounding 9 per cent, while the real interest rate was something like 3 per cent. This meant that little entrepreneurial skill was needed to make a handsome return on investment. The tide was rising quickly and lifting all boats, while the cost of borrowing money was very low. To quote a businessman at the time, 'Any fool can make money nowadays'. Now that this situation has been changed so drastically, the incentive to invest is no longer very strong. Potential investors – entrepreneurs – will have to be a lot braver in the future. Unfortunately, a relatively high proportion of them have little knowledge of investing in anything other than property. These entrepreneurs are not going to make much of a contribution to the economy for several years.

Concluding Comments

It is not obvious that our innate behaviour as entrepreneurs, consumers and employees will impart a significant boost to the indigenous economy in the years ahead. We certainly have the ability to do better, but usually only for specific tasks and for relatively short periods of time.

The present recession will be a test of our mettle. It is likely that we will suffer more than most other countries – and for longer – and there is a danger that confidence will be eroded. This risk seems all the greater because the optimism of the Celtic Tiger period has already turned into a disabling form of depression.

Many younger people have never experienced even a mild recession and seem to be genuinely shaken by such a sharp downturn coming at a time when they are severely saddled by debt – a problem which will be made much more severe by the cost of bailing out the banks. The sharp increase in suicide rates to very high levels is a tragic consequence of the downturn.

It seems as if consumers are able to adjust their behaviour more radically than the other groups who operate on the supply-side of the economy. This is worrying because if consumer demand shrinks, and at the same time the production of goods and services remains sluggish, then it is hard to see where the growth momentum will come from in the longer term. Rising export markets are a possibility, but only if we manage to restore our competitiveness.

We still have a significant infra-structural deficit, especially in relation to public transport and broadband, and the National Development Plan will have to be severely curtailed to reduce the fiscal deficit over the next three years. Governments always find it easier politically to cut capital spending rather than social welfare and public sector pay. Investment in human capital will also remain inadequate. These factors, allied with competitiveness difficulties and a serious debt overhang, will undermine longer-term growth. Thus, a modest 2 per cent trajectory for the indigenous economy may be regarded as rather optimistic.

9

CAN WE DO BETTER?

'Emergencies have always been necessary for progress....
It took a depression to show us the value of a job.'
– Victor Hugo

As a society we may be satisfied with a modest growth rate of 2 per cent per annum over the next fifteen to twenty years. If, for example, we decide not to make more effort economically, but to concentrate more on artistic, spiritual or leisure pursuits, then so be it. Such social choices must be respected. People determine the economy; it's not the other way around, nor should it be. But if we are not satisfied with the prospect of a modest 2 per cent increase in real living standards, what could we do to improve it? Since there are probably no soft options left, the question should be reformulated as: what are we prepared to do for a higher rate of economic growth – something approaching 4 per cent per annum? It is important to note that the difference between a 2 per cent and a 4 per cent growth trajectory can be quite substantial over a long period. For example, allowing for compounding, the lower growth rate would result in a cumulative increase in real living standards of 35 per cent after 15 years. The higher growth rate, however, would deliver an increase of 80 per cent over the same period.

There would also be substantial differences in job creation and unemployment under each scenario.

It is possible to make suggestions about how to achieve the higher growth rate – and the rest of this chapter attempts to do so – but our culture-induced behaviour of the past would indicate a strong reluctance to change, even if good leadership were provided. In the 1960s we were on a growth path of 4 per cent but that was coming from a low base at a time of buoyant world trade. Between 1995 and 2007 we had significantly higher growth rates without having to change our behaviour all that much because the dynamism came from US multinationals and interest rates, which were far too low. But in the future, if we want to move on to a 4 per cent growth path (without the benefit of new FDI), then we will have to change in fundamental ways.

Helping Entrepreneurs

Entrepreneurs will need to improve in relation to decision-making, risk-taking and the assumption of responsibility. Their role in the economy is of enormous significance since they organise most of the other factors of production. But they can no longer rely on cosy cartels, tax breaks, subsidies for R&D, insider information, access to politicians, positions of market dominance, asymmetric information and the preferential award of contracts. They must recognise that growth was too easy in the past – with all the easy options of cohesion funds, low profit tax, coat-tailing on the backs of multinationals or reproducing goods and services invented by others. They should be prepared to take on a much tougher competitive environment and one that is far more demanding in terms of technological innovation and original research. The government, of course, is still searching for more easy options, for example tapping into the diaspora,

commercialising Irish culture, attracting Islamic banking into
the International Financial Services Centre. The reality is that
the days of strokes and 'cuteness' are over. Accountants and
auditors now have fairly demanding compliance codes and can
no longer cut corners or engage in irregularities – to use one of
their euphemisms for dishonesty.

Nor should emerging entrepreneurs fear loss of face in the
event of one or two failures. They must rise above narrow and
inhibiting social mores and have the courage of their convictions; they should dare to fail. From time to time they will need
to throw caution to the winds, refuse to be deflected from their
ambitions, and let the adrenalin flow. Of all the forms of renewable energy, adrenalin is the most important; it sweeps away the
inhibitions of history. The problem in the past was one of will
rather than one of ability.

There is a sort of fallacy of composition to be overcome. A
potential entrepreneur might think, 'If the indigenous economy
is going to grow by only 2 per cent, then it is going to be very
difficult to get a good return on capital. Why should I bother?'
Of course, if all individuals think like that, then no initiatives
will be taken. This is where leadership comes in. If government
could convince emerging entrepreneurs that if they began to invest in their businesses the growth rate could be doubled, then
the return on investment would be more than adequate. The
bodies that represent the business sector also have a part to play
in this regard. These bodies, as well as the trade unions, spend
too much time lobbying government and dividing up the national cake, rather than trying to increase its size and improve
its quality. They complained bitterly about the failure of banks
to lend to their members, even after the creation of NAMA, but
why did they not set up a special bank to help their member

companies? Direct company-to-company lending is not un-common in other countries.

One of the big unknowns is whether or not the future system will be a capitalist one. This must be a source of uncertainty for the business community. Obviously Ireland will follow the lead shown by the US, but it is not yet clear to what extent President Obama will restore the machinery of capitalism after its disastrous collapse in 2008.

In the absence of convincing leadership, it will be more difficult for individuals to make entrepreneurial decisions. But if a few show courage, it is likely that others will follow their lead. The problem is how to get the ball rolling. There are incentives of a sort in a recession, such as cheaper properties, lower prices for capital goods and a less congested infrastructure. Government incentive schemes may help at the margin, but these should not be too generous because they might not attract the right kind of entrepreneur, who by definition has to be a self-starter.

The rewards for genuine entrepreneurship should be as high as the market will bear. Salary caps may be appropriate in banking but not where productive, risk-taking enterprise is concerned; it is this which generates employment. A clear distinction between entrepreneurship and rent-seeking must be drawn.[1] If genuine, tough and imaginative entrepreneurs emerge during this recession, they will deserve the respect of their communities and so will move up the social pecking order. The day may come when parents will boast about having an entrepreneur rather than a doctor (or a priest!) in the family. This day may come sooner than we think, as entrepreneurship becomes more and more associated with innovation and the smart economy, and less conflated with 'Taigs in trade'.

More mechanisms must be found to build bridges between research centres and entrepreneurs. Researchers in Trinity College Dublin are on the brink of finding a cure for leukaemia; it will be interesting to see if this remarkable development will be commercialised in Ireland or if the ideas will be sold to international companies. Ireland has in the past produced great scientists but for some reason the culture has been less welcoming towards enterprise. The Higher Education Authority confirmed in late 2009 that the engagement of industry with third- and fourth-level research facilities is poor. This should be redressed immediately.

There needs to be an overhaul of corporate governance and of the penalties for non-compliance. It is relatively easy to enforce rules, but that will not make entrepreneurs any more dynamic. The rules should be carefully formulated so as to foster genuine enterprise and not to inhibit it with excessive red tape. State agencies should give every encouragement to young entrepreneurs. It is unlikely that our main banks are going to act as venture capitalists for first-time entrepreneurs in high-tech businesses that bankers would not understand. We need much more business experience in the Department of Enterprise, Trade and Employment and, indeed, in politics as a whole.

To the extent that entrepreneurship can be taught, it should be put on the school curriculum. The subject should emphasise those areas of greatest weakness, such as decision-making under uncertainty, alertness to opportunity, marketing, innovation and interpersonal skills. The current teaching of business does not cover these aspects in sufficient detail. Teachers should be encouraged to stream children who show entrepreneurial flair; teachers themselves may need to be educated in this respect. In fact, parents have an important part to play in helping their children to learn from their mistakes and lose the fear of failure, to which they may be predisposed. Oddly enough, fear of success may also inhibit enterprise, if young people feel unworthy about achieving their ambitions.

There may be merit in setting up an institution specialising in entrepreneurship, where second-level and third-level students could supplement their existing studies. It is very important for science and technology students to familiarise themselves with key aspects of entrepreneurship. This would help bridge the gap – a wide one in Ireland – between good research ideas and their commercial implementation. It is not unusual for engineers to move into managerial positions, but, to date, not many scientists have set up their own businesses.

Various projects have been proposed as possible niches that could play to Ireland's strengths. Commentators have, for example, proposed organic food, fresh fish (both of which would conform with our 'green' image), environmental goods and services, including energy substitutes, and financial and business software. Energy substitution seems to be essential for a country like Ireland which has little fossil fuel and which has turned its face against the nuclear option – with little or no discussion. As a fall-back position, we should perhaps develop inter-connectors to import nuclear energy from the UK. There are some encouraging signs that our natural resources of wind, tides, waves and bio-fuels are beginning to be exploited. Some observers believe that business and financial services would be a useful niche to pursue. These are all helpful proposals and in most of these sectors we might well have a comparative advantage that has not yet been exploited. But we cannot engineer these outcomes. It is up to entrepreneurs to grasp such opportunities and exploit them.

Conventional wisdom seems to indicate that manufacturing is now an 'old economy' activity that has fallen from favour.

When Britain was in the process of de-industrialisation in the 1970s and thereafter, there were many disparaging references to manufacturing, sometimes dubbed 'thing-making'. Later on in the yuppie era, Britain concentrated, perhaps to an unhealthy degree, on financial services. It is obvious that in Ireland we have priced ourselves out of traditional manufacturing in comparison to low-wage countries like China and India. But we should be careful not to throw out the baby with the bath water. Richard Dyson, for example, has re-engineered several existing products and made them much better. Good design will always be in demand, and, as the German economy continues to prove, excellence in engineering always has a market. We need to adopt a diversified approach to the supply-side of the economy and not concentrate unduly on IT services.

Reforming Government and the Public Sector

Government and the public sector are in need of major reform. Rather than hire gurus to impose systems from the top down, it is vital to bring people along with the process of reform; otherwise it will not work. Irish people have generations of experience of wriggling out from under imposed constraints. At political level, incentives will have to be 'rebalanced' to encourage work in the national interest, rather than for short-term political gain. Competence rather than popularity will have to become the main criterion for election to high office. People-pleasing and what psychologists call 'adaptive plasticity' will have to be replaced by firm, enlightened leadership. Ministers should be tested much more rigorously by journalists and interviewers on a routine basis. At the present time, many ministers refuse to appear on programmes where they are likely to be shown up by astute questioning.

Ministers sometimes admit in private that they got something wrong, but they will rarely say so in public. This Protean behaviour is a mistake even from a narrow political perspective. The electorate would actually admire a politician who admitted mistakes in public or in a formal setting, such as a television discussion programme. They would come across as much more human. If senior politicians took the risk of 'being themselves' more often, they might well unearth true leadership qualities. President McAleese made a slip of the tongue in a speech some years ago, and then apologised immediately without any reservation. It was a sincere apology and she went even higher in people's estimation. Politicians have a lot to learn from her.

The tradition in Ireland of appointing people to the boards of public bodies without any reference to ability will have to cease. This is a dreadful custom because it enshrines mediocrity. The boards so appointed often refer to their political mentors for advice. This allows politicians the opportunity of influencing events by stealth without having to take any responsibility for their actions. It is strange that political appointees allow themselves to be used in this manner. This machine for perpetuating inefficiency must be dismantled and replaced by a system of genuine open competition. Only in this way can we ensure that wasteful expenditure – of the order of €4-5 billion a year – will be eliminated. In short, the entire public sector apparatus must become a meritocracy, from top to bottom. Genuine reform on this scale will take years to implement and there will be resistance every step of the way. We should not vote for any party that does not promise to abolish political appointments.

At present many well-connected – and indeed well-meaning – people float from one board meeting to another without drawing breath, eating excellent lunches in corporate restaurants, not entirely sure which company they happen to be in at any given time. Sometimes they can make a contribution by virtue of their domestic and external contacts. They socialise with their friends, promise to meet again in a month or so, and move on to the next board meeting.

Part of the problem with this system is that it has demoralising trickle-down effects. Most people working in an organisation will know that the directors were appointed for political reasons. Consequently, their leadership ability will not be respected by the staff. Moreover, it is natural for staff to infer that networking and the correct party affiliation are the only 'skills' required. Politicians have never understood the corrosive aspects of this system. Doing favours for individuals does a huge disfavour to the economy, and to society as a whole. When a former Taoiseach, Bertie Ahern, stated openly on television that he appointed friends to the boards of public bodies, no political party even questioned the practice. Yet it is likely that this practice contributed to the property bubble, the failure of regulation and the collapse of the financial system. Any politician who is genuinely concerned about the economy and determined to create jobs for people should seek to outlaw political appointments at the earliest opportunity.

Ministers will have to learn how to make tough decisions and deal with difficult trade-offs, where one group of people may benefit but only at the expense of another group. They require the courage to make unpopular decisions in favour of the national interest. The government has claimed credit for taking tough budgetary decisions. Fair enough, but remember there was no alternative. Brussels was breathing down their necks and the international capital markets and credit rating agencies made it clear that Ireland would find it difficult to borrow on reasonable terms. When NAMA is fully up and running, the government will have more scope to borrow from the Irish banks. It will be interesting to see if, in those circumstances, it will continue the process of fiscal adjustment, especially as the next general election gets closer.

The approach adopted by the New Zealand government in the late 1980s is one that could be followed here in the future. When bringing in painful economic reforms, the New Zealand government adopted a sequential approach which helped to win the acceptance of the whole community. Thus, when farmers were up in arms having lost certain agricultural subsidies, the government announced the withdrawal of grants to industry, and so on. Each sector realised that all other sectors were sharing the pain of the adjustment in equal measure. This kind of approach is *essential* in Ireland because the withdrawal of existing benefits has a disproportionate psychological effect on those concerned. At present, it is difficult to think of any sector – teachers, electricians, gardaí, nurses, recipients of children's allowances, higher civil servants, old-age pensioners, car salesmen, restaurant-owners – who do not regard themselves as victims who have to bear most of the burden.

Prevention is infinitely better than cure in Ireland. It was extremely foolhardy for governments here to lavish benefits on people in good times because it is next to impossible to take them away when the economy weakens. No new expenditure programme should ever be contemplated unless there is a clear statement about where the money to finance it is going to come from. One has only to think of the withdrawal of the medical card from elderly people and the extraordinary reaction it provoked, even among people who were quite well off. The measure was perceived as a personal affront. A similar response is evoked by imposing small charges on public services that were once provided free. Populist governments which provide bread and circuses to the electorate in good times do enormous harm to the economy.

The public sector's performance in creating physical infrastructure has been poor. There is an urgent need for large-scale projects to be subjected to rigorous cost-benefit analysis and the required skills will have to be provided as soon as possible. This desideratum applies with equal force to the intellectual infrastructure – broadband, property rights, computers in schools – which must underpin the smart economy.

Transparency is essential in a modern democracy. We must turn our backs on the hypocritical approach of 'opaque transparency' which we adopted in the past. With this mindset, public officials were schooled in the black arts of answering parliamentary questions so as to give the impression of being forthcoming while concealing the important information. Many politicians and public officials still adopt the 'bikini' approach to information: they reveal as much as they can while concealing the important bits. Since the various tribunals of inquiry revealed compromising documents prepared by public officials, there has been a reluctance to put written material on file or even on computer. Where it was necessary to write something, 'post-its' were used; these can be detached and 'mislaid' as required. This sort of behaviour is inimical to transparency, efficiency, accountability and democracy.

The Tallaght strategy of 1987 under which the Fine Gael leader, Alan Dukes, promised not to oppose the minority Fianna Fáil government as long as it followed a path of fiscal rectitude, was a courageous decision and, unfortunately, the political system was not mature enough to reward the author of the strategy. In fact, he was punished by losing the leadership of his party. This reflects badly on our political system. At the present time there is much discussion about a non-partisan national government to find the best way out of the current crisis. It is unlikely to happen, however, because the pull of the old-fashioned adversarial system is too strong. Nor is it clear that the opposition parties want to take responsibility for difficult decisions.

Hype and spin should never again be substituted for substance, and all public relations and style gurus (including cosmeticians) should be struck off the public payroll immediately. The hundred or so civil servants who are assigned to work on ministerial constituency business should be allowed to return to their proper duties. Politicians should try to live in the real world, not the Forbidden City of Leinster House, and they should use public transport instead of helicopters. Irish electorates would have far more respect for politicians if they did not behave as an elite group or an ascendancy class. As mentioned above, the media has an important role to play in forcing politicians to face the important issues of the day and in keeping them grounded. It would be highly beneficial if, from time to time, expert ministers of state were appointed.

The costs of running the Houses of the Oireachtas should be halved and Seanad Éireann should be abolished. The number of TDs and ministers of state should be reduced, as should the number of ministerial advisors, constituency workers and assorted hangers-on. At least half of the Dáil and Seanad committees should be abolished and the chairpersons of the remaining half should surrender their perks and privileges. Only the Taoiseach should have a car and driver. Salaries of all politicians should be reduced by at least 20 per cent and no pensions should be paid to politicians while they are working. It is clearly absurd that the Taoiseach is one of the world's highest paid heads of government. Politicians should demonstrate that they operate in the national interest and not for themselves. I once ventured this opinion to a senior political figure, who pointed out that, 'once we got the British out, it was our turn to get our snouts in the trough'.

It is essential that ministers take a much more diligent approach to public spending and tax evasion. This could save a staggering €4-5 billion a year, and satisfy the need for fiscal consolidation without deflationary tax increases or cuts in legitimate spending programmes.

We have to get away from the local constituency approach which has led to soul-destroying clientelism. Over the years this has led to a trivial form of government where the role of the legislator is diminished. Since the foundation of the state, only forty private member bills have been introduced in the Dáil. Much legislation is not adequately debated and often ends up full of loopholes and inconsistencies which invite challenges in the courts. Improving government requires a fundamental change to some form of list system and to the adoption of single-seat constituencies. If we are serious about acting in the national interest, this change is essential. People would no longer depend on largesse from their local representatives; this is the best – perhaps the only – way of 'releasing the genius of the people' and inculcating a general self-reliance. We have had many situations where politicians behaved badly and were rightly criticised in the national press, only to be absorbed into the bosom of their local constituencies and re-elected with generous majorities. Without forgiving, well-nursed constituencies to fall back on, politicians would have an incentive to behave better.

Reforming the political system would also have the effect of attracting able young people into politics. The fact that George Lee attracted such a huge vote suggests that many people are dissatisfied with the tired old faces that appear nightly on their television screens. Unfortunately, he left politics after nine months on the grounds that he was unable to make a contribution to economic policy. Although the details have not been fully revealed, it is hard to avoid the conclusion that politics, like most other sectors of Irish society, is resistant to change, to fresh ideas and to new people. In Ireland, everyone is expected to serve a long apprenticeship and work their way up in an organisation; the idea of some wunderkind being fast-tracked is anathema to us. This is as true of politics as it is of industry or the public service.

Democracy is not in a healthy state in Ireland. The 2007 general election led to a coalition and a hastily cobbled together programme for government for which nobody had voted! It came to light in March 2010 that the Green Party wanted to rotate their ministers at mid-term and may have had a secret agreement to this effect with Fianna Fáil. Recently the leader of the Labour Party, Eamon Gilmore, was asked whether and how his party might coalesce with Fine Gael. If such a coalition were to be formed, surely it would be essential to present the combined programme for government to the electorate *before* the election. Eamon Gilmore seemed genuinely puzzled by the question. Given his personal popularity and the massive swing to Labour in the polls in June 2010, it seems likely that Labour will form a substantial part of the next government. Mr Gilmore could even be the next Taoiseach. It is possible, therefore, that we will again end up with a coalition policy programme for which nobody voted. It might also be mentioned in passing that social partnership was fundamentally anti-democratic because the social partners did not represent the electorate and yet had an important say in economic and social policy. During the final, ill-fated series of meetings on pay cuts, a union representative informed a reporter that they, the social partners, were engaged in very important work and that the public should keep out of it. The mask slipped.

Most governments tend to support the existing establishment which includes producers, banks and property owners (but not consumers or taxpayers). Indeed the main parties are fairly centrist ones – perhaps reflecting the innate conservatism of the country. Apart from library sit-ins, there was very little radicalism in Ireland in the post-1968 period – except of course for the civil rights movement in Northern Ireland. It is interesting to reflect on how the establishment responded just before the financial collapse in 2008. The Minister for Finance and his department, the Central Bank and Financial Regulator, all the CEOs of the banks and a firm of consultants assured us that there was no problem, that the banks had ample capital and capacity to meet any future contingencies. The establishment closed ranks to protect itself. It was completely untrue and when the collapse occurred, everything was done to protect the establishment. Consumers and taxpayers were ignored because those groups are not part of 'official Ireland' and are not organised. Even if NAMA were reasonably well designed (which it isn't), most people do not believe the projections underlying it. What it will do is transfer resources from taxpayers to shareholders and bondholders. The legal profession will also gain substantially. The establishment will win yet again.

This major inequity is at the heart of the present social confrontation. There may be merit in trimming social welfare spending and the pay of many workers, but against the background of NAMA and the protection of the banks, these adjustments are regarded as unacceptable and have led to major confrontations. We need superb leadership to mediate between the factions, but, unfortunately, we do not have it. And bodies like the National Economic and Social Council and the National Economic and Social Development Office have not helped. A task force set up in 2009 to study growing unemployment met only once in nine months! The government does not seem to be unduly concerned about unemployment, but neither does Fine Gael. In July 2010, when very worrying Live Register figures appeared, Fine Gael became embroiled in a struggle for the leadership of the party.

Of the 850 public bodies, quangos and task forces – many with political appointees – about half should be disbanded or merged over the next few years. The Department of Health and Children, for example, has 88 different bodies reporting to it. Do we really need separate bodies to deal with health insurance, seafood safety, food safety, human medicines, veterinary medicines, poisons, fluorides, alcohol and tobacco control, and so on? Many public bodies were set up for cosmetic reasons and to 'outsource' (that is, dodge) decision-making, which should be returned to ministers and their departments where it belongs. Indeed, if civil servants were more involved in decision-making, it would greatly improve their morale.

The rest of the public sector should be asked to carry out a zero-based budget review. It is likely that this would lead to substantial savings. An alternative might be to put most public sector bodies on a four-day week. It is possible that the 20 per cent cost saving might even result in higher output per person. No government department or public body should engage consultants or legal counsel without ministerial permission, and then only in exceptional circumstances. Civil servants should have the confidence to write reports and offer advice themselves.

In the early phase of the present recession, the logistics of paying social welfare to increased numbers of unemployed workers came under strain. The immediate reaction of government was to recruit more officials to deal with such work. Because of slack in other parts of the public sector there is no need for this. It is simply a matter of reallocating existing resources.

There should be major transfers in any case. For example, public officials should be moved from the Department of Agriculture to the IDA, from the Departments of Health and Foreign Affairs to the far more important functions of competition, regulation and consumer affairs. There should be much sharper focus in our embassies on attracting business to Ireland. Specially qualified business and economics graduates, trained by the IDA and by Enterprise Ireland, should be assigned to our embassies in the ten most advanced countries – in place of diplomats and administrators. Indeed, it might be preferable to replace the Irish Embassy in every important capital city by an 'Ireland House' which would represent every aspect of Ireland, from industry to diplomacy, from culture to tourism. This kind of one-stop shop – which would be cost-effective and synergistic – would give a clear signal that Ireland was open for business. To give effect to necessary transfers and changes of focus, public officials would need to be retrained. We should no longer assume that up-skilling is required only in the private sector. A limited version of this kind of mobility and flexibility was on offer by trade unions in exchange for a reversal of pay cuts, just before social partnership collapsed in 2009. Under the terms of the Croke Park agreement, much the same offer by the unions is still on the table, but the reversal of pay cuts has been replaced by a promise not to impose additional cuts in the future. Only time will tell the exact shape of that agreement; there is likely to be slippage and fudge on both sides.

The emphasis should be on policy-related work. Perhaps the original *aireacht* idea, discussed earlier, should be examined afresh, though it could be implemented only by bringing fresh talent into the public sector. What we must not do is give practically all executive functions to a public-sector body, such as the HSE, retain the legacy department, in this case the Department of

Health and Children, and pretend that the legacy department concentrates on policy. This is nothing more than *ex post* rationalisation. Instead of policy initiatives being proposed, what usually happens is that the legacy department spends most of its time monitoring and interfering in the work of the executive body. The *aireacht* idea, however, may never be implemented because it tends to be equated with the notion of an intelligentsia, something that is anathema to Irish people – and certainly to existing civil servants, who would regard it as a blockage to promotion.

Assessment and benchmarking of the outputs of the public sector should be regularly carried out. The payment of annual increments should no longer be regarded as automatic, but a reward for special merit. Bonus schemes should be dropped because they were never properly related to performance.

A former Taoiseach, Garret FitzGerald, has written about poor skill levels in government departments. He noted that the Department of Finance employed only three economists and that the revenue forecasting ability of that department was extremely poor. In his view, the department did not learn from its mistakes – which was 'unacceptable'.[2] Since this is the premier department of the public service, what must the others be like? In many ways the Central Bank and the office of the Financial Regulator were unduly influenced by the Department of Finance, and by their own boards of political appointees. The culture was a deeply conservative one. I am always intrigued by the symbolism of the sculpture in the Central Bank plaza. There is a cowl of cut stone protecting a tree of gold. Is it the nation's wealth which is being protected or a golden circle? At one point during the process of choosing a sculpture for the plaza, the selection committee was greatly impressed by a sculpture of Icarus falling from the sky, his wings in disarray. This sculpture was turned down because it might have been taken to symbolise the banking system!

Within the public sector, promotion will have to be based on merit rather than seniority (or political compatibility). Merit should be broadly defined to include initiative and innovation, which are conspicuously lacking at present. Highly qualified experts should be attracted into government departments even if they have to be paid more than secretaries general. The present unwritten rule that administrators should be paid more than experts should be abolished. (Imagine running a health service if top medical consultants with fifteen years of third- and fourth-level training could not be paid more than HSE managers!)

There would be merit in bringing private sector people into the public sector. The US practice of transferring high profile people into the Treasury, Fed and State Department should be adopted, though not on the basis of political affiliation. The Department of Finance and the Financial Regulator require more economic expertise. Other departments, and government itself, would benefit from people with business experience.

Because of a steady politicisation of the public sector, there has been no source of truly independent advice for government. Senior advisors of the same political hue will tend to tell the minister what he or she wants to hear. There is also a sort of tribal imperative that everyone should sing from the same hymn sheet, thus preventing honest and vigorous debate on every issue. This desire for homogeneity at all costs discourages fresh thinking.

The Economic and Social Research Institute should be asked to spearhead a long-term economic plan, in the preparation of which they would liaise with business people, policy-makers, consumers and employees. They should also consult with sociologists and experts in cultural studies, because in many instances, strategies that look good on paper may not be implemented properly if the people involved are hostile to them. This explains why so many 'reforms' in the past ended up causing resentment rather than efficiency gains. Policies should play to people's strengths. The plan would integrate the public finances, tax reform, spending cuts and public sector reform into the macro-economy. Special attention should be paid to the indigenous economy, and the help of the Central Statistics Office may be required to separate out this part of the overall economy – to the extent that this is possible, even on the basis of broad estimates. An important aspect of the plan would be a set of manpower forecasts which would give some idea of the skills likely to be required over the future decades. It would also be necessary to undertake policy simulations or 'what if' scenarios to help the government examine different strategies; this dimension has been conspicuous by its absence over the last twenty years. Following the recent difficulties in the financial sector and the reputational damage caused by Ireland's banks and status as a tax haven, it will be necessary to re-visit the question of the rapid growth expected in the financial sector. A good deal of research will be necessary to see if this sector will be quite as dynamic after the recent financial collapse.

An issue that merits considerable attention relates to competitiveness. Ireland cannot grow without exporting. More research should be done on developing better indices of competitiveness and of market shares. Although the euro has been weak because of problems relating to Greece, this may not always be the case. In the longer term, if China loses faith in the US dollar, it is possible that the euro would rise too much against the dollar and perhaps against sterling as well. If the euro continued to rise against the dollar, this would be a problem not just for Ireland but for many other countries as well. The IMF should re-examine the proposal of a substitution account. This is an account based on the Special Drawing Right – an international currency created by the IMF. Countries like China with surplus dollars could substitute them in this account, rather than selling them in the market and driving down the dollar exchange rate. The ESRI and Central Bank should develop this idea with a view to tabling it for discussion at the appropriate international fora.

More economic research is also required on the implications of EMU membership for a country like Ireland. Are there other policies that can be substituted for the loss of interest rate and exchange rate policies? Given the differing structures of the member economies, what steps are needed to ensure that the Eurozone becomes an optimal currency area? One idea which deserves investigation is a unit-cost pact between members. In other words, whenever a member country begins to lose competitiveness, it would be noted by the European Central Bank and measures would be taken at an early stage to correct the problem, before exchange-rate pressures came to the fore.

The ESRI plan should tackle the supply-side as well as the demand-side of the economy. The notion of industrial clusters or growth poles should be studied in consultation with the IDA and Enterprise Ireland – and in the context of the national spatial strategy. The recent research merger between TCD and UCD should be broadened to include all the third-level and fourth-level institutions. Since scientists are not usually entrepreneurs, special attention must be given to ways of commercialising ideas so as to increase value-added at home.

Fine Gael has advocated the creation of a super semi-state body that would subsume several of the existing ones. There might be merit in this idea but only if the attitudinal reforms described above are carried through. New institutions run by the same people, appointed in the usual uncompetitive manner, will not deliver the goods. In fact, as matters stand, the rivalry that would be generated between the new and the old institutions would probably stultify the whole enterprise. Once again, the 'people' aspect is crucial.

Government and the public sector must learn that it is vitally important to keep something in reserve for a rainy day. The government did at least have the National Pension Fund to fall back on for recapitalising the banks, but it should have had a much larger reserve accumulated on the basis of windfall tax revenues during the boom years. Governments will have to learn not to discount the future too heavily. Electorates will have to learn to see through the gimmickry of populist handouts.

It is very important for government and the public sector to maintain credibility. If the electorate comes to believe that the government is incompetent or unaccountable, or too close to builders and bankers, then we could be facing civil unrest, in which case the economy would suffer for a very long time. The Irish economy is already being bracketed with the poorer performers of the Eurozone – Portugal, Italy, Greece and Spain – formerly called the 'Club Med' countries but now dubbed PIGS, an unfortunate acronym. There is a danger that the Eurozone could split into a two-tier system; there has been considerable discussion of forming a European Monetary Fund – along the lines of the IMF – to help the lagging countries. At present we stand at a crossroads. The government, its advisors and senior administrators seem overwhelmed by the recession and the banking crisis. It is a worrying time.

In trying to consolidate the fiscal situation, the government has to get the balance right between deflationary impulses and deficit reduction. In an open economy we have seen that fiscal changes do not have very strong effects on demand, but they are not negligible. If the two 2009 budgets and the 2010 one cause significant deflation or civil unrest, the government may have to rethink its strategy, regardless of pressure from Brussels, and consider the less conventional options proposed in the last chapter.

Parts of the public sector are well run, for example the parks section of the OPW, the Criminal Assets Bureau, the national museums and art galleries, the Labour Relations Commission and the Oscar-winning Ballyfermot College of Animation. It is important to study the success stories. At first glance, the best-run parts of the public sector appear to be those where the work involved is stimulating and fits well with our national characteristics. The real challenge, of course, is to improve performance in those sectors that do not have these natural advantages. Managers need to become more familiar with job-enrichment methods.

Empowering Consumers

A much greater focus on consumer rights is required to make up for years of neglect. The group that includes consumers also takes in taxpayers and for years they have been treated badly by governments, possibly because they do not give donations to political parties in the way that enterprises do. The other reason consumers and taxpayers are ignored is because they are so amorphous, almost invisible. Contrast this with trade unions, for example, where we can immediately visualise people like Jack O'Connor or David Begg. When we think of consumers or taxpayers, who comes to mind? Nobody.

Consumers were never represented in the tent of social partnership and had no voice. It is not surprising that they are subject to very high stealth taxation and, more recently, levies. With unemployment soaring and national disposable income shrinking, consumers are going to have to retrench for several years to come. Firms providing luxury goods and 'discretionary' services will be hardest hit.

To the extent that there is a 'wealth effect' in Ireland, it is likely that consumer behaviour will tend towards caution. It was one thing to spend when the value of property and equities was rising continuously; it is another matter to spend when asset prices collapse. The negative wealth effect is compounded by a negative income effect caused mainly by substantial job losses, but also by higher taxes and levies. It is no surprise that the demand for new cars and foreign holidays has collapsed. The scrappage scheme will do little other than change the timing of car purchases.

Consumers may retrench even more than might be expected because they have bad memories of having been gouged and treated shabbily during the boom years. An overreaction might also occur because of uncertainty. There is considerable discussion about additional taxation to come in 2011 and in subsequent years. Allied to the uncertainty about job security and the adequacy of pensions, there is now a climate of austerity, analogous to that which influenced the previous generation of farmers. Future economic policy – ad hoc rather than planned – is now as unpredictable as the Irish weather.

With national output falling dramatically, consumers may now realise how artificial the good years were. Because of the influence of multinational companies, we had decent jobs and incomes which we did not really create for ourselves. We now realise that it will not be so easy in the future. This reality check may also mean a further constraint on spending.

Where consumers are concerned, it is difficult, maybe irrelevant, to be prescriptive. In principle, it would of course help the economy to weather the storm of recession if consumers were to increase spending. But people will themselves decide how much to spend and how much to save. If they feel confident about the future, they will tend to spend more, other things being equal. But it would be wrong to use public relations techniques to persuade consumers to spend more. Confidence must be based on reality. If government and the public sector were reformed, and if the results of reform were visible, there could be a boost to confidence and a much-needed stimulus to consumer spending.

The Competition Authority and National Consumer Agency will have to do far more to prioritise the rights of consumers and to improve the functioning of markets in general. I have brought four different malpractices to the attention of the NCA and been rebuffed each time; there has been no investigation or follow-up. Every issue raised was deemed to be 'outside the remit of this agency'. Other people have had similar unhelpful experiences. Ombudsman's offices are also dismissive of complainants except in extremely dramatic cases which they usually bring to the attention of the media to create a good impression. There would be merit in putting one minister in charge of these offices, all forms of regulation and the restoration of competitive markets. If consumers were organised, they could test the various public bodies that are supposed to have their best interests at heart. In other words, consumers could act as 'phantom shoppers', contacting the various agencies and reporting on the responses. In Ireland, unfortunately, we have to 'guard the guardians'. As noted earlier, consumer spending accounts for over 50 per cent of GNP and yet it does not 'rate' a government department. Yet agriculture, which accounts for 2 per cent of GNP, has its own dedicated government department with over 4,000 staff!

Consumers should organise themselves into a lobby group. This would enable them not just to improve their own welfare, but also to act as quality controllers. They should constantly be giving signals to Irish producers about how they ought to improve their products and services, and/or reduce their prices. This quality-controlling function is vital for a country that has to depend on export markets to survive. If a company cannot satisfy its own consumers, it is not going to have much success abroad. In Ireland, most of our exports come from multinational companies based here. In future we will have to depend much more on indigenous companies. Highly organised and demanding consumers are essential for preparing Irish companies to break into export markets.

By the same token, if the quality and price of domestic products satisfy consumers, then they will buy more from the domestic market. Otherwise they will import more, use the internet, or go north of the border or to New York. As consumers, we may not complain much but we do vote with our feet. The single European market and a more global world economy provide us with many more optons than we had in the past. Those who argue that we should be patriotic and 'buy Irish' are unwittingly ignoring the quality-control function which is of vital national importance.

There is a large sheltered sector in Ireland into which the forces of international competition do not easily penetrate. Apart from the public service, many of the professions are in this sector – bankers, lawyers, doctors, dentists, architects, engineers. Their fees and charges are much too high and add to the costs of doing business in Ireland. These professions need much tougher forms of regulation and meaningful sanctions. Self-regulation or principles-based regulation is no longer appropriate.

Following the banking fiasco, it is time to consider a different form of financial regulation, one where the sanctions for breaches of rules would be punitive, and where banks themselves would have to contribute to a self-insurance fund. The latter would put the banks in a position to bail themselves out in the event of any future catastrophe. This would obviate the need for taxpayers' funds in the future, force the banks to become more efficient and thereby eliminate the problem of moral hazard. Consideration might also be given to a special tax or levy on banks over and above the one envisaged in the NAMA legislation, which will probably be passed on to the consumer anyway. There is no need to increase the number of staff engaged in regulation. Once the system has been reformed and tightened up, there could be substantial staff savings.

Neither should we fear the possibility of the banks being taken over by foreign companies. The only difference this would make would be to eliminate the costs of regulation in Ireland! There are no New Zealand-owned banks and those that do business in New Zealand are regulated by their home countries. In the light of recent events, that sounds like a satisfactory arrangement. Before we joined the Eurozone there may have been some merit in having 'Irish' banks because monetary policy was conducted with the cooperation of the banks. But since monetary policy has been hived off to the ECB in Frankfurt, this argument loses whatever force it may have had.

Recognising the Worth of Employees

Despite recent demonstrations in the streets, employees and unions deny that the issue is about pay cuts and levies, emphasising that it is about fairness. There is a perception that the super-rich are getting off scot-free and that the burden of adjustment is being borne disproportionately by the poorer sections of society. This is largely true and it is a major source of annoyance to many people. The super-rich have ways of sheltering income from taxation, many of them legal. Tax exiles have to spend half of the year outside of Ireland but no one can check on this since they have their own executive jets and can come and go as they please; it is doubtful if they provide much employment in Ireland. The government will have to close off as many of these loopholes as possible.

The government has imposed a cap on the salaries of the CEOs of the participating banks. If this were extended to other senior executives in the banks, it might bring a perception of equity into the situation, though it is unlikely to satisfy workers and trade unions. It is interesting to note in passing that in the good years the market mechanism was regarded as sacrosanct. Now, following the implosion of the banks, governments in capitalist economies have no qualms about controlling wages!

It is worth noting that the budgets in 2009 and 2010 hit the middle class very hard. For example, the top marginal tax rate was increased by 9 percentage points, setting at nought the idea that high taxes are bad for initiative. Most middle-class employees will be affected by these taxes and levies, and since they are the backbone of the country it is likely that the disincentive effects will damage the economy. The prospects of additional taxation, possibly including a property tax, to come in 2011 and thereafter, will undermine confidence. Middle-class workers do not usually demonstrate in the streets, but they react in other ways. We should not be surprised to see some degree of capital flight and a new brain drain. This is another risk of fiscal consolidation – on top of the deflationary one.

There is a pressing need to improve science education at all levels so that employees will be skilled and adaptable enough to remain productively in the labour force. Professor Ferdinand von Prondzynski, former president of Dublin City University, has argued that primary schools neglect essential preparation for mathematics and science, and secondary schools adopt poor teaching methods and turn students off science and technology. He also believes that the points system often leads to students following careers that do not suit them. One improvement that comes to mind involves special incentives for science teachers, following the American system. It is possible that good science teachers should command salaries up to twice those earned by their colleagues. In return, these teachers would be expected to submit to regular inspection and evaluation.

In early 2010 evidence came to light about grade inflation at secondary and tertiary level. It came from two sources: the CEOs of a number of multinational companies expressed concern about the falling problem-solving ability of new recruits who had been awarded good honours degrees. In addition, researchers at the Tralee Institute of Technology showed that in many third-level courses the proportions of first-class and upper second-class degrees had risen enormously. This is a serious development and strikes at the heart of our economic future. The educational sector will have to be subjected to the closest scrutiny and revamped from top to bottom. FÁS, the state training agency, will have to be included in that structural reform. In March 2010, the Minister for Education stated that industry should be more involved in setting educational standards. No doubt, many educators will object on the grounds that training people for industry is too far removed from Cardinal Newman's idea of a liberal education. This is one of the big choices that society will have to make. If we want faster economic growth, then we may have to devote fewer resources to liberal education.

It is necessary to downgrade, relatively speaking, the salaries available to bankers, lawyers, accountants, and other professionals whose contribution to job-creation and to the 'smart' economy is quite limited, or non-existent. The free market might bring about this result if professional cartelisation were prevented by a more proactive Competition Authority.

The law should be changed in favour of employers. At present it is too easy for inefficient employees to win suits for unfair dismissals. It is demoralising for productive workers to see lazy colleagues benefiting from the present system. Generally speaking, labour law needs to be upgraded and enforced to prevent vexatious and nationally damaging industrial relations disputes. In April 2009, an unofficial strike in Dublin Bus left 150,000 commuters stranded each day. The Irish Business and Employers Confederation (IBEC) requested that the army be called out. Later that year taxi-drivers brought the centre of Dublin to a standstill without any intervention by the police. Since then we have had frequent demonstrations in the streets and go-slows in the public sector. Trade unions do not seem to realise how such demonstrations, flashed around the world, can frighten away potential job-creating inward investment and nullify our preferential tax regime.

Corporate law should also be changed to prevent the abuse of limited liability and to enable more sanctions to be applied to white-collar criminals. The government has promised a consolidated corruption bill which would also provide protection for whistle-blowers. A legal services ombudsman may also be appointed. It will be interesting to see how these initiatives work out in practice. There are powerful vested interests against such reforms.

Since Irish people do not really like hierarchical structures and because, historically, there was no deep-seated class system in Ireland, there would be merit in introducing profit-sharing schemes in certain industries on an experimental basis. This is not a new idea, but it is one that has been too readily dismissed in the past – partly because of our resistance to change. Trade union leaders are wary of this system because it might lessen their role. Some employees believe they would be cheated under such a system. Employers claim that workers would take their share of profit in the good times but would be reluctant to share in the losses whenever these occurred. None of these objections is grounded in fact. The idea that profit-sharing schemes would lead inexorably to socialism is also wide of the mark. Profit-sharing schemes are a pragmatic approach to exploiting our strengths and our values as a community living on a small island.

Profit-sharing would empower workers and give them a stake in the firm they work for. Management would have to consult them about policy changes. Managers might be reluctant to share power at the beginning, but they would get used to it in time. The approach is worth trying on an experimental basis, especially when jobs are being lost in many different companies. If it worked, there is every reason to expect higher productivity. Indeed, it is hard to imagine that Waterford Glass would have collapsed if workers had been consulted on a regular basis over the years.

Profit-sharing, the key to the 'third way' between capitalism and socialism, would restore the crucial link between productivity, wages and profitability, which has been conspicuously absent for years. It would encourage workers to be more flexible with regard to work practices since they would essentially be working for themselves. Each worker could decide, within limits, on the work-life balance that best suited their circumstances. It would also allow us, as a society, to dismantle the cumbersome, time-wasting and undemocratic machinery of social partnership, from which workers, taxpayers and consumers are barred. It would encourage genuine personal interaction in the workplace. Profit-sharing might well be the vehicle that could transport the traditional *meitheal* concept across the divide from agriculture to industry and services – a concept that developed organically and which embodied the basic values of the community. It is strange that this cooperative model which worked so well in agriculture was not adopted more widely in other sectors of the economy. It is likely that we are unduly influenced by the organisational structures of the US and UK and simply applied them to the Irish economy without regard to our own cultural values. These structures were, however, a poor fit and did not lead to the 'coincidence of interests' that we find in the leading economies of the world. The boss/worker nexus is more difficult to manage in Ireland than in other countries. In many ways the distinction between entrepreneur and employee is artificial; we are all producers in the same way that farmers are. Profit-sharing would play to our strengths, help morale and the work ethic, and improve productivity.

Although most public sector bodies do not make profit as such, the concepts underlying profit-sharing could still be adopted. For example, a flatter structure could be substituted for the existing hierarchical one, and mechanisms could be introduced to involve 'junior' officials in policy-making at national and departmental levels. All this presupposes that key departments of state – and their ministers – would once again take responsibility for matters that have been outsourced to quangos and consultants over the years.

A more equal society would be likely to emerge without in any way reducing the incentive to invest and make profit. Greater equality would lessen the possibility of industrial relations difficulties which in the past have earned Ireland a poor reputation abroad and which are likely to repeat themselves at the worst possible time. It is not being suggested that profit-sharing be imposed on multinational companies since they belong to a different culture.

There will always be unemployed people and it is important that support mechanisms are in place to prevent them from falling into despair. It is especially important to eliminate the discouraged worker syndrome from inner cities where it has become all too prevalent. When the sons and daughters of unemployed people find themselves unemployed, it can become self-perpetuating. This vicious cycle must be broken. High unemployment among young males is associated with increased crime and drug-taking. It is no surprise that the number of head shops had increased rapidly in the last couple of years, at least until the government brought in controls.

It is important to save existing jobs. Economists might argue that the process of creative destruction necessarily implies job losses in certain sectors and job creation in others. While this is true, it should be remembered that when jobs are lost, it can lead to hysteresis, loss of tax revenue and increased government spending. If at all possible and without propping up lame duck industries, greater efforts should be made to save existing jobs. In a system of profit-sharing, there would be consultations with the employees, and wage-cuts and other forms of cost reduction could be hammered out together. Employees, for example, would have a say in whether profit margins (or wages) should be reduced to make the business more competitive.

Shared decision-making would allow employees scope for making their jobs more interesting. Top-down schemes are never going to be as successful as those brought into being by the people themselves. A share economy would be a true social partnership, as opposed to the mutant version that existed until 2010. All the individual stakeholders become empowered and 'them and us' attitudes wither on the vine. In short, the differences between the economy and the community would begin to disappear. All this may be regarded as fanciful or quixotic, but it is difficult to envision a substantially improved performance without such a qualitative change in the way people – employees and entrepreneurs – work together. A share economy would be consistent with a genuine republic, as distinct from the sort of tribal elitism that has been the norm since the foundation of the state.

Concluding Comments

Irish people will determine their economic future. As matters stand, there is not much prospect of a quick ending to the recession or of expanding the indigenous economy at a rate above some 2 per cent per annum over the longer term. If we are content with that and do not wish to alter our present behaviour, then so be it. Fundamentally, it is society's choice. If people are more interested in artistic pursuits, for example, then they should not be coerced into commercial activities. What we must not do, however, is refuse to change behaviour and yet aspire to more dynamic growth. That way lies frustration and discontent, made manifest in economic terms by inflation and loss of competitiveness.

There is always the possibility that world economic preferences will change in such a way as to play to our strengths. This would be the ideal. We could grow faster by doing what we love and getting paid for it. To some extent, IT-related activities fall into this category. While we would have been alienated by assembly-line production, we rather like working with computers. This is a note of hope for the future. Of course the chances of world preferences changing to match up perfectly with our cultural needs are fairly remote and we should not pin our hopes on such a 'rub of the green'.

To achieve a higher growth path of 4 per cent, say, would require fundamental changes in the way we do business, on the part of entrepreneurs, employees, consumers and the public sector, including government. These changes may be too much to ask. If we are happy with more slowly rising living standards, then it may not be worth changing merely to do better in the future when we are already reasonably well off. This is one of the choices that should be widely debated, because there is no point in trying to change behaviour if it involved too great an effort. It is suggested here that the share economy would be a natural fit, given our history and culture. Given the failures of capitalism in recent years it would not be surprising if other countries were also seeking a middle way.

Governments invariably assume – or pretend – that we can have higher economic growth without having to change our behaviour; we can eat our cake and have it too. This may have been true to some extent in the past when several soft options were available, but it is almost definitely a false premise at the present time and is likely to remain so for the foreseeable future.

More rapid growth does have other advantages in addition to boosting living standards. A high-performing economy gains the respect of the world and increases the country's voice in international fora. In Ireland's case it might also improve the prospects of a united country at some stage in the future. There can be little doubt that the Celtic Tiger era contributed in some degree to parity of esteem and the peace process.

We could also choose to have more equity in the system. This might reduce the chosen growth path to some extent, partly because progressive taxation would lessen incentives. But if society regards that as a reasonable trade-off, then so be it. There may also be a trade-off between economic growth and protecting the environment. Again, the precise balance to be found between both these worthy objectives will be a matter for society to establish.

Whatever growth path is chosen, we should try to ensure that growth is soundly based. In other words, it should not be based solely on consumer spending fuelled by borrowing. In the longer term that kind of development will not prove sustainable. We must prioritise investment- and export-led growth which is harder to achieve. So, in this sense too, the soft option of credit-driven consumption must be moderated, and entrepreneurs must accept greater challenges.

Estimates made in September 2010 suggest that the burden of debt resulting from bank bail-outs could absorb over 1.5 per cent of GDP each year for the next decade. This represents a new and daunting challenge to the community.

It will not be easy to set aside the inhibiting influences of history and culture. If, however, we can overcome our reluctance to change – as entrepreneurs, policy-makers, consumers and employees – and are prepared to undertake much-needed reforms, including improved governance at macro and micro levels, we might be able to push the long-term growth rate (of the indigenous economy) from 2 per cent to about 4 per cent per annum. As noted, this would mean that, over a fifteen-year period, we could improve real living standards by about 80 per cent (instead of 35 per cent) even without additional American investment. Such a solid economic performance would reduce unemployment and emigration, improve the quality of health and education, and provide adequate pensions for older people and a secure future for the young. But if we cannot, or do not really wish to change the way we conduct the ordinary business of life, then we will have to content ourselves with a much more modest economic future. The choice is ours.

NOTES

Introduction

1. Lawrence Harrison, *The Central Liberal Truth*, Oxford University Press, 2006. E.L. Jones, 'The Revival of Cultural Explanation in Economics', *Economic Affairs*, Vol. 23, No. 4, 2003.

2. Pete Lunn, *Basic Instincts: Human Nature and the New Economics*, Marshall Cavendish Ltd., 2008.

3. Declan Kiberd, *Inventing Ireland*, Harvard University Press, 1997. Richard Kearney, *The Crane Bag, Journal of Irish Studies* (1977-85). Fintan O'Toole, *The Ex-Isle of Ireland: Images of a Global Ireland*, New Island Books, 1997.

4. Ronan Fanning, *Independent Ireland*, The Educational Company of Ireland, 1990. Joseph Lee, *Ireland 1912-1985: Politics and Society*, Cambridge University Press, 1989.

5. Niall Ferguson, *The Ascent of Money: A Financial History of the World*, Allen Lane, 2008.

6. G. Akerlof and R.J. Shiller, *Animal Spirits*, Princeton University Press, 2009.

1 The Human Factors of Production

1. R. Goosen, *Entrepreneurial Excellence: Profit from the Best Ideas of the Experts*, Career Press, 2007.

2. C. Antonelli, *New Frontiers in the Economics of Innovation and New Technology: Essays in Honour of Paul A. David*, Edward Elgar Publishing, 2006. R. J. Gordon, 'Does the New Economy Measure up to the Great Inventions of the Past?' National Bureau for Economic Research Working Papers, 2000.

3. Fintan O'Toole, *Ship of Fools*, Faber and Faber, 2009.

2 Components of the People Economy

1. J.M. Keynes, *The General Theory of Employment, Interest and Money*, Cambridge University Press, 1936.

2. The Commission of the European Communities et al, System of National Accounts, 1993.

3. The distinction between gross domestic product (GDP) and gross national product (GNP) is not referred to in this chapter. GNP is actually a truer measure for Ireland because the repatriated profits of multinational companies are deducted from this measure.

3 Unusual Features of the Irish Economy

1. Kearney, *op. cit.*

2. Lunn, *op. cit.*

3. Francis Fukuyama, *Trust: The Social Virtues and the Creation of Prosperity*, Simon and Schuster, 1966 and *The End of History and the Last Man*, Avon Books, 1993.

4. The film *Wall Street* (1987) starring Michael Douglas as Gordon Gekko.

5. Adam Smith, *An Inquiry into the Nature and Causes of the Wealth of Nations*, Edinburgh, 1776. See also Adam Smith, *The Theory of Moral Sentiments*, Edinburgh, 1759.

6. IMF Article IV Consultation with Ireland, Public Information Notice, September 2007.

7. There are a few reasons why budgets in Ireland have rarely been used to manage aggregate demand. The Department of Finance has such a poor record of forecasting revenue that it is difficult to build in a policy dimension. The openness of the economy is sometimes put forward as a reason, in that a government stimulus, say, would leak away via increased imports. There is also the argument that if a budget did give more purchasing power to consumers by lowering taxes, for example, people might not spend much of their windfall but instead put it against the probability of taxes being raised again in the future. The book-keeping (as opposed to policy) approach was underlined by finance minister Charlie McCreevy when he said, in 1998, that he would spend more if he had the revenue, and vice versa.

8. G. Lowenstein, *Exotic Preferences: Behavioural Economics and Human Motivation*, Oxford University Press, 2007.

4 How Entrepreneurial Are We?

1. Edward de Bono, *Why So Stupid? How the Human Race Has Never Really Learned to Think*, Blackhall Publishing, 2003.

2. Lee, op. cit.

3. Lee, ibid.

4. Tom Garvin, *Preventing the Future: Why Was Ireland So Poor for So Long?* Gill and Macmillan, 2005.

5. Assuming that begrudgery is still part of our national 'make-up', it is important to suggest that it is not always a bad quality. In a sense, it is a safety valve that prevents the rise to high office of someone suffering from paranoid delusions. He or she would quickly be 'cut down to size' for entertaining notions of grandeur. Arguably, in the 1930s, Germany did not have such a safety valve.

6. Terry Eagleton, *The Truth about the Irish*, New Island Books, Dublin, 2002.

5 The Underperforming Public Sector

1. P.C. Nutt, 'Comparing Public and Private Sector Decision-Making Practices', *Journal of Public Administration Research and Theory*, 2006.

2. While it might be hoped that commercial state enterprises would make profit, this is not always the case, and bodies like Dublin Bus depend on considerable state subsidies.

3. OECD, Ireland: *Towards an Integrated Public Service*, Paris 2008.

4. From a Keynesian perspective, fiscal policy should have been counter-cyclical so as to put more spending power into the economy at times of sluggishness, and vice versa.

5. Garret FitzGerald, *Reflections on the Irish State*, Irish Academic Press, 2003. In this book, the former Taoiseach says of the Department of Finance, 'there is now a most serious shortage of skills, especially of economic skills at the Assistant Principal level where much research and policy analysis takes place. This may perhaps account for the stark deterioration in

the quality of revenue forecasts and also in the control of public spending. The error of €2 billion in the calculation of the tax revenue that the correctly estimated GNP figure would yield in 2001 is horrifying, and the failure either to explain why this happened or to announce any action to prevent a recurrence is simply unacceptable.'

6. OECD, op. cit.

7. J. Casas-Pardo, and M. Puchades-Navarro, 'A Critical Comment on Niskanen's Model', *Public Choice*, Vol. 107, 2001.

8. Devlin et al., *Public Service Organisation Review*, Dublin 1969.

9. C. Buchanan and Partners, *Regional Development in Ireland*, Dublin 1968.

10. M. Bahmani-Oskooe and D. Rhee, 'Time Series Support for Balassa's Productivity-bias Hypothesis', *Review of International Economics*, Vol. 4, 1996.

11. OECD, op. cit.

6 Passive Consumers

1. When Bobby Sands died on hunger strike in 1981, many Irish people were badly shaken. American colleagues of mine could not understand the reaction. Their view was that if he wanted to die, it was his choice. Later, in a taxi in a small Caribbean country, the taxi-driver and his friend were trying to figure out where Ireland was. They asked me some questions and conferred among themselves. Then one of them said. 'Yes, the country of Bobby Sands.' To them he was a hero, much like Che Guevara. The reactions of people in different countries can be poles apart, reflecting different cultural values.

2. T. Prone, *Mirror, Mirror: Confessions of a Plastic Surgery Addict*, Sitric Books, 2001.

3. D. Ricardo, *On the Principles of Political Economy and Taxation*, London, 1817.

4. Lowenstein, op cit.

7 Insecure Workers

1. R. D. Atkinson, *The Past and Future of America's Economy*, The Information, Technology and Innovation Foundation, Washington DC, 2004.

2. W.A. Fleckenstein, *Greenspan's Bubbles: The Age of Ignorance at the Federal Reserve*, McGraw-Hill, 2008.

3. M. Leon-Ledesma and P. McAdam, 'Unemployment, Hysteresis, and Transition,' Royal Economic Society, 2003.

4. T.K. McCraw, *Prophet of Innovation: Joseph Schumpeter and Creative Destruction*, Harvard University Press, 2007.

5. 'Building Ireland's Smart Economy: A Framework for Sustainable Economic Renewal', Dublin, 2009.

6. G. Colvin, 'Layoffs Cost More Than You Think', *Fortune*, March 2009.

7. D. Ariely, *Predictably Irrational: The Hidden Forces that Shape our Decisions*, HarperCollins, 2009.

8 Ireland's Growth Prospects

1. 'Building Ireland's Smart Economy', op. cit.

2. E. Wirter and C. Kraldau, 'Competition to Innovate Among Industrialised Nations: Key Results', The German Institute for Economic Research, Berlin, 2007.

3. 'Facing the Challenge: The Lisbon Strategy for Growth and Employment' (the Kok Report), a publication of the European Communities, November 2004

4. D. Sul and P.C.B. Phillips, *The Elusive Empirical Shadow of Growth Convergence*, Cowles Foundation, Yale University, 2003.

9 Can We Do Better?

1. Rent-seeking is a form of semi-parasitic behaviour whereby an individual or group of individuals extract value from others without compensating them adequately. Rent-seekers, by definition, have low productivity and contribute little if anything to society as a whole. See A. Krueger, 'The Political Economy of the Rent-Seeking Society', *American Economic Review*, 1974; G. Tullock, *The Rent-Seeking Society*, George Mason University, 2005.

   Those who believe that banking in Ireland is genuine entrepreneurship, devoid of parasitic behaviour, should read *Bankers*, Shane Ross, Penguin Ireland, Dublin, 2009.

2. Fitzgerald, op. cit.

INDEX

086 833 8772